Charles Portales Golightly

The Position of the Right Rev. Samuel Wilberforce

Lord Bishop of Oxford, in Reference to Ritualism...

Charles Portales Golightly

The Position of the Right Rev. Samuel Wilberforce
Lord Bishop of Oxford, in Reference to Ritualism...

ISBN/EAN: 9783744763387

Printed in Europe, USA, Canada, Australia, Japan

Cover: Foto ©ninafisch / pixelio.de

More available books at **www.hansebooks.com**

THE POSITION

OF THE

RIGHT REV. SAMUEL WILBERFORCE, D.D.

LORD BISHOP OF OXFORD,

IN REFERENCE TO RITUALISM.

THE POSITION

OF THE

RIGHT REV. SAMUEL WILBERFORCE, D.D.

LORD BISHOP OF OXFORD,

IN REFERENCE TO RITUALISM,

TOGETHER WITH

A PREFATORY ACCOUNT

OF THE

ROMEWARD MOVEMENT IN THE CHURCH OF ENGLAND
IN THE DAYS OF ARCHBISHOP LAUD.

BY

A SENIOR RESIDENT MEMBER OF THE
UNIVERSITY OF OXFORD.

" The thing that hath been, it is that which shall be; and that which is done is that which shall be done: and there is no new thing under the sun." *Eccles.* i. 9.

LONDON,
HATCHARD AND CO. 187, PICCADILLY;
SLATTER AND ROSE, OXFORD.
1867.

BAXTER, PRINTER, OXFORD.

A PREFATORY ACCOUNT,

&c.

TILL Mr. Hallam published his Constitutional History of England, but little was accurately known of the Romeward movement in the Anglican Church during the earlier half of the seventeenth century.

That Archbishop Laud was inclined to a few mediæval superstitions, and persecuted the Puritans who objected, among other outward observances, to the use of the Surplice, and to making the sign of the cross at Baptism,—and further, that the Pope had offered him a Cardinal's hat,—was about as much as could be gathered from the pages of Hume, and the more popular writers of English history; but that serious and systematic efforts were made, like those which we witness in our own day, to undo the work of the Reformation, and negotiations actually entered into with Papal emissaries for a reunion of the Churches of England and Rome, are facts of history which will probably even now be a surprise to the general reader. The following extracts however, from some of our leading historical writers, will go far to put him in possession of the state of the case.

Lord Clarendon[a] thus describes the earlier phase of the movement :

" Though the nation generally had no ill talent to the Church either in the point of the doctrine or the discipline, yet they were not without a jealousy that popery was not enough discountenanced, and were very averse from admitting any thing they had not been used to, which they called innovation, and were easily persuaded that any thing of that kind was but to please the papists.

" The remissness of Archbishop Abbot, and of other Bishops by his example, had introduced, or at least connived at, a negligence that gave great scandal to the Church, and no doubt offended very many pious men. The people took so little care of the churches, and the parsons as little of the chancels, that, instead of beautifying or adorning them in any degree, they rarely provided against the falling of many of their churches; and suffered them at least to be kept so indecently and slovenly, that they would not have endured it in the ordinary offices of their own houses[b]; the rain

---

[a] History of the Rebellion, Book i.

[b] William of Wykeham had complained of the like slovenliness nearly 300 years before. He had observed, he said, in his several visitations, that the sacramental plate and cloths of the altar, surplices, &c. were sometimes left in such an

and the wind to infest them, and the Sacraments themselves to be administered where the people had most mind to receive them. This profane liberty and uncleanliness the Archbishop (Laud) resolved to reform with all expedition, requiring the other Bishops to concur with him in so pious a work; and the work sure was very grateful to all men of devotion: yet, I know not how, the prosecution of it, with too much affectation of expense, it may be, or with too much passion between the ministers and the parishioners, raised an evil spirit towards the Church, which the enemies of it took much advantage of as soon as they had the opportunity to make the worst use of it[c].

uncleanly and disgusting condition, as to make the beholders shudder with horror,—" quod aliquibus sint horrori";—adding, that it seemed quite preposterous to omit in sacred matters that attention to decent cleanliness, the neglect of which would disgrace a common convivial meeting. See White's Selborne.

[c] The Church building and Church restoring movement of our own day began long before the rise of Ritualism. From the Report of the Census of 1851, it appears that of the 14077 then existing Churches, Chapels, and other buildings belonging to the Church of England, there were built

<pre>
        Before   1801 9667
        Between 1801 and 1811   55
        .... 1811 and 1821   97
        .... 1821 and 1831 276
        .... 1831 and 1841 667
        .... 1841 and 1851 1197
        Dates not mentioned 2118
</pre>

"The removing the communion table out of the body of the Church, where it had used to stand, and to be applied to all uses, and fixing it to one place in the upper end of the chancel, which frequently made the buying a new table to be necessary; the enclosing it with a rail of joiner's work, and thereby fencing it from the approach of dogs, and all servile uses; the obliging all persons to come up to those rails to receive the Sacrament, how acceptable soever to grave and intelligent persons who loved order and decency, yet introduced first murmurings among the people upon the very charge and expense of it; and *if the minister were not a man of discretion and reputation to compose and reconcile those indispositions, (as too frequently he was not, and rather inflamed and increased the distemper,) it begot suits and appeals at law.* The opinion that there was no necessity of doing any thing, and the complaint that there was too much done, brought the power and jurisdiction, that imposed the doing of it, to be called in question, contradicted, and opposed. Then *the manner, and gesture, and posture in the celebration of it brought in new disputes, and administered new subjects of offence according to the custom of the place and humour of the people: and those disputes brought in new words and terms, (altar, adoration and genuflexion, and other expressions,) for the more perspicuous carrying on those disputations. New books were written for and* against this new practice with the same earnestness and contention for victory, as if the life of Christianity had been at stake. BESIDES, THERE WAS NOT AN EQUAL CONCURRENCE IN THE PROSECUTION OF THIS MATTER AMONGST THE BISHOPS THEMSELVES; those who had been preferred by the Archbishop's favour, or hoped to be so, being at least as solicitous to bring it to pass in their several dioceses, some of them with more passion and less circumspection[d] than they had his example for, or than he approved; others proceeding more remissly in it, and not only neglecting to direct any thing to be done towards it, but restraining those that had a mind to it from meddling in it. AND THIS AGAIN PRODUCED AS INCONVENIENT DISPUTES, WHEN THE SUBORDINATE CLERGY WOULD TAKE UPON THEM, NOT ONLY WITHOUT THE DIRECTION OF, BUT EXPRESSLY AGAINST THE DIOCESAN'S INJUNCTIONS, TO MAKE THOSE ALTERATIONS THEMSELVES, AND BY THEIR OWN AUTHORITY.

"Though there were books written with good learning, which fully vindicated the proceedings which had been carried on, yet it was done by men whose names were not much reverenced, and who were taken notice of, with great insolence

---

[d] Lord Clarendon attributes the mistakes of the Bishops, among other causes, to their ' receiving for the most part their informations and advertisements from Clergymen, who understand the least, and take the worst measure of human affairs of all mankind that can write and read.' Life, vol. i. p. 74.

and asperity, to undertake the defence of all things which the people generally were displeased with, and who did not affect to be much cared for by those of their own order. So that from this unhappy subject, not in itself of that important value to be either entered upon with that resolution, or to be carried on with that passion, proceeded upon the matter a schism among the Bishops themselves, and a great deal of uncharitableness in the learned and moderate Clergy towards one another, which, though it could not increase the malice, added very much to the ability and power of the enemies of the Church to do it hurt, and also to the number of them. For without doubt many who loved the established government of the Church, and the exercise of religion as it was used, and desired not a change in either, nor did dislike the order and decency which they saw mended; yet they liked not any novelties, and so were liable to entertain jealousies that more was intended than was hitherto proposed; especially when those infusions proceeded from men unsuspected of any inclinations to change, and were known assertors of the government both in Church and State."

That the 'jealousies' which Lord Clarendon here refers to, as entertained by others besides the Puritans, were only too well founded, he was very well aware. But he had said enough for his purpose, which was to shew the immediate causes which led to the overthrow of the established Church; and he had no occasion to go into further particulars respecting the Romeward movement. His silence is the less to be regretted, that Mr. Hallam, in the following passages of his 'Constitutional History[e],' has put us in possession of all, that we could want to know, from other sources of information:

"The charge of inclining towards popery, brought by one of our religious parties against Laud and his colleagues with invidious exaggeration, has been too indignantly denied by another. Much indeed will depend on the definition of that obnoxious word, which one may restrain to an acknowledgment of the supremacy in faith and discipline of the Roman see; while another comprehends in it all those tenets which were rejected as corruptions of Christianity at the Reformation; and a third may extend it to the ceremonies and ecclesiastical observances which were set aside at the same time. In this last and most enlarged sense, it is notorious that all the innovations of the school of Laud were so many approaches in the exterior worship of the Church to the Roman model. Pictures were set up or repaired; the communion-table took the name of an altar, it was sometimes made of stone; obeisances were made to it; the crucifix was sometimes placed

[e] Vol. i. chap. viii. The first edition of the Constitutional History was published in 1827.

upon it; THE DRESS OF THE OFFICIATING PRIESTS BECAME MORE GAUDY; churches were consecrated with strange and mystical pageantry. These petty superstitions, which would of themselves have disgusted a nation accustomed to despise as well as abhor such pompous rites, became more alarming from the evident bias of some leading churchmen to parts of the Romish theology. The doctrine of a real presence, distinguishable only by vagueness of definition from that of the Church of Rome, was generally held. Montagu, Bishop of Chichester, justly reckoned the chief of the Romanizing faction, went a considerable length. towards admitting the invocation of saints; prayers for the dead, which lead naturally to the tenet of purgatory, were vindicated by many; in fact, there was hardly any distinctive opinion of the Church of Rome, which had not its abettors among the Bishops, or those who wrote under their patronage. The practice of auricular confession, which an aspiring Clergy must so deeply regret[f], was frequently inculcated as a duty. And Laud gave just offence by a public declaration, that, in the disposal of benefices, he should, in equal degrees of merit, prefer single before married priests."

[f] Mr. Hallam means to intimate, that the Romanizing party in Archbishop Laud's days regretted that auricular confession, as an instrument of putting power into the hands of the Clergy, had been abandoned at the Reformation.

"It is alleged by one who had much access to Laud, that his object in these accommodations was to draw over the more moderate Romanists to the English Church, by extenuating the differences of her faith, and rendering her worship more palatable to their prejudices[g]. There was, however, good reason to suspect, from the same writer's account, that some leading ecclesiastics entertained schemes of a complete reunion; and later discoveries have abundantly confirmed this suspicion."

The discoveries referred to by Mr. Hallam are due to the publication, at the close of the last century, by a Romish priest of the name of Berington, of the memoirs of Gregorio Panzani, an emissary of Pope Urban VIII. at the Court of Charles I. The information furnished by this work, now not easily to be met with, is in the highest degree curious and interesting.

It would appear from this narrative, that the project of a reunion originated with two of Charles' ministers, Secretary Windebank and Lord Cottington, both secret Romanists, who entered into negociations with Panzani; and that to these negociations the Bishop of Chichester, already referred to (Montagu), soon made himself a party. In a private interview he immediately entered upon the subject of a reunion, expressing to

[g] Heylin's Life of Laud, p. 390.

Panzani a great desire that the breach between the two Churches might be made up, and assuring him that he apprehended no danger from publishing the scheme as things now stood. He said that he had frequently made it the subject of his most serious thoughts, and had diligently considered all the requisites of a reunion; adding, that he was satisfied that both the Archbishops, with the Bishop of London, and several others of the episcopal order, besides a great number of the learned inferior Clergy, were prepared to fall in with the Church of Rome as to a supremacy *purely spiritual;* that for his own part he knew no tenet of the Church of Rome to which he was not willing to subscribe, unless it were the article of Transubstantiation, which word he had reason to think was invented by Pope Innocent III. after the Council of Lateran had risen. He owned he had some scruples concerning communion in one kind; but as for particular points, he thought the best method would be to choose moderate men deputies on both sides, to draw up the differences in as small a compass as they could, and confer about them.

In subsequent interviews with Panzani, Bishop Montagu, after repeating what he had said about the reunion, added that he was 'continually employed in disposing men's minds for it both by words and writing as often as he met with an opportunity.' He then again mentioned the Pope's supremacy, whose feet he said he was willing to kiss, and acknowledge himself to be one of his children. Upon Panzani's remarking to him that the union, if it were to take place, must not only be politic and ceremonial, but real and in *unitate fidei,* without any admixture of creeds, the Bishop assured him that he aimed at a total union.

On two occasions the Bishop asserted, in conversation with Panzani, the validity of Anglican orders[h], maintaining that they were derived from St. Augustine, the apostle of England, though he was sensible that the writers of the Church of Rome made little account of Anglican ordinations. Panzani evaded the question, observing that it was a tedious, intricate controversy, with the particulars of which he was not acquainted. "The Bishop remarking, that the king had been often heard to say that there was neither policy, christianity, nor good manners in not keeping a correspondence with Rome by sending and receiving ambassadors, as was practised by other Courts; and that if His

[h] The writer of an article in 'The Church and the World,' headed 'Reunion of the Church,' gives an entirely erroneous account of these negociations, and seems never to have heard of Mr. Berington's work. According to him, 'the quarrel to be reconciled was between the two *Courts* of England and Rome, *not between the two branches of the Church;*' and he remarks, that 'there is no trace in the discussions with Panzani of any doubt having arisen of the validity of Anglican orders'!

Majesty should think fit to settle such a correspondence, he would himself make interest for that honourable charge;" "Then," replied Panzani, "the world would immediately conclude that you were going over to the Church of Rome." "And what harm would there be in that?" said the Bishop. Panzani, once more referring to the reunion, expressed himself in a very desponding manner, considering the many difficulties with which they had to struggle. "Well," said the Bishop, "had you been acquainted with this nation ten years ago, you might have observed such an alteration in the language and inclinations of the people, that it would not only put you in hopes of an union, but you would conclude it was near[i] at hand." Then he solemnly declared that both he, and many of his brethren, were prepared to conform themselves to the method and discipline of the Gallican Church, where the civil rights were well guarded. "AND AS FOR THE AVERSION (i. e. to Rome) WHICH WE DISCOVER IN OUR SERMONS AND

---

[i] Exaggerated language of this kind is characteristic of the Romanizing party of our own day; e. g.

"We are met with the objection,—as long as Rome remains as it is, and England remains as it is, reunion is impossible. This is a truism, but we may fairly question the premisses. The facts stated shew that *there is an incredible change in the religious mind of England within the last twenty-five years. What may it not be in the next quarter of a century?*" The Church and the World, p. 200.

PRINTED BOOKS, THEY ARE THINGS OF FORM, CHIEFLY TO HUMOUR THE POPULACE, AND NOT TO BE MUCH REGARDED."

The falsehood and dishonesty which Bishop Montagu pleads guilty to in the foregoing sentence would throw doubt upon the whole of his previous statement, were it not in the main confirmed by other testimony. Mr. Hallam remarks, that "it appears almost certain that Montagu made too free with the name of the Archbishop, and probably of many others." With respect to Laud himself, it must be borne in mind that he made this solemn declaration on the scaffold: "This is no time to dissemble with God, least of all in matters of religion; and therefore I desire it may be remembered, I have always lived in the Protestant religion established in England, and in that I come now to die." But it cannot be doubted that there were other Bishops, who owed their preferment to Laud, of the same mind with Montagu. Of Goodman, Bishop of Gloucester, it is remarked in Panzani's Memoirs, that "of those of the Episcopal order, none appeared more zealous for union with Rome; and that he every day said the priest's office, and observed several other duties, as practised in the Church of Rome." Yet of this very Bishop, Heylin remarks in his Life of Laud, (p. 263.) that "having staid in his diocese long enough to be as weary of them as they were of him, he affected a remove to the see of Hereford, and had *so far prevailed with some great officer of State, that his money was taken*, his congé-d'élire issued out, his election passed. But the Archbishop coming opportunely to the knowledge of it, and being *ashamed of so much baseness in the man who could pretend no other merit than his money*, so laboured the business with the King, and the King so rattled up the Bishop, that he was glad to make his peace, not only with the resignation of his election, but the *loss of his bribe*." He died a Romanist.

It would not be proper to conclude this account without some notice of the Tract XC. of its day, a work entitled 'Deus, Natura, Gratia;' the production not, as in the case of Mr. Newman's publication, of a Protestant Clergyman, but of a Franciscan friar, Father Davenport, otherwise called Franciscus à Sancta Clara. It was an attempt to reconcile the statements of the Thirty-nine Articles with Romish doctrines, " the usual trick," Mr. Hallam observes, "of Popish intriguers." King Charles I. is said to have been pleased with it, but it was far from being liked at Rome, where it was considered to make too great concessions to the Protestants. It was put in 'the Index,' like Dr. Pusey's Eirenicon.

Some reports of the negociations with Panzani reached the ears of the public, and no doubt served to increase the general uneasiness. But nothing excited so much alarm as the perpetual perversions[k] to the Romish faith. "These had not been quite unusual in any age since the Reformation, though the balance had been very much inclined to the opposite side. They became, however, under Charles, the news of every day; *Protestant Clergymen* in several instances, but *especially women of rank, becoming proselytes* to a religion so seductive to the timid reason and susceptible imagination of that sex." At last all was thrown into confusion, the Bishops expelled from the House of Lords and deprived of their revenues, the use of the Liturgy prohibited, and the National Church overthrown. *Absit omen!*

"THE THING THAT HATH BEEN, IT IS THAT WHICH SHALL BE; AND THAT WHICH IS DONE IS THAT WHICH SHALL BE DONE: AND THERE IS NO NEW THING UNDER THE SUN."

[k] It is almost needless to remark, that many of the perverts to Rome in our own day have been from the same classes of the community; e.g. the Duchesses of Buccleuch and Argyle, the Marchioness of Lothian, the Ladies Feilding and Campden, &c. &c. The writer has lying before him a list of between eighty and ninety clerical members of his own University who are now in the Church of Rome.

THE POSITION OF THE BISHOP OF OXFORD IN REFERENCE TO RITUALISM.

IT will be readily admitted that the Bishop of Oxford is at the present moment the most prominent ecclesiastic in England. To say nothing of his energy and ability in the administration of his diocese, his powers of public speaking give him the lead among his episcopal brethren in the Upper House of Convocation and the House of Lords. His personal influence exercised in private is very great, and is brought to bear with peculiar effect on the Church in the Colonies. One of his favourite Clergy has been recently appointed to the Bishopric of Calcutta; he has induced the Archbishop of Canterbury to join with him in recommending another to the Bishopric of Natal. No doubt he looks forward to the time, and with no unreasonable expectation, when his influence will be greatly increased, and possibly through his instrumentality great changes be effected in the position of the National Church.

It is a question then of no little importance, How does he stand affected towards that great movement, which is causing so much agitation at the present time, and which goes by the name of Ritualism?

The appointment of the Very Rev. Samuel Wilberforce, Dean of Westminster, to the See of Oxford, took place immediately after the secession of Mr. Newman to the Romish Communion in the autumn of 1845; and his first measures gave promise of a very effective Episcopate. Whilst kind and conciliatory to all with whom he came in contact, he made the most friendly advances to those of the Clergy, whose sentiments were most in accordance with those of his honoured father; designated himself to the writer of these pages, if his memory does not deceive him, as an Evangelical High Churchman; and wished it to be understood, in reference to Mr. Newman's followers, that he was 'decidedly opposed to that party.' How far he was disposed to carry his opposition, it would perhaps startle some of the leaders of that party to learn; but upon that subject the writer's lips are sealed.

A Sermon delivered in Christ Church Cathedral at his first General Ordination, (Dec. 21, 1845,) contained admirable advice to the Clergy. It is 'on our knees,' he told them, 'if any where we learn to love the souls of our people; to hate our own sins; to trust in Him who shews us then His wounded side and pierced hands, and to love Him with our whole heart. Nothing will make up for the lack of prayer. The busiest ministry without it is sure to become shallow and bustling.'

Not less valuable is the following, in the same strain, from his Primary Charge in 1848:

"We want for the ministry of our parishes earnest spiritual men; men of prayer, men of faith, men of God; men who can 'speak what they do know, and testify what they have seen;' men who can witness to others of the salvation that they have found themselves; who can speak of Christ as having known Christ; who can declare the Spirit's power, because He has wrought upon themselves; to whom the Church of the redeemed is not a name or an abstraction, but the living company of Christ's saints, amongst whom He lives and walks, who is their soul's desire and happiness: men to whom the doctrine of the Sacraments is not a ground for wrangling, or a cold, hard formulary of orthodoxy, but a discipline and fount of life. And for this, above all other needs, a holy, devout, faithful life is needful in ourselves; that in all our treatment of others we may be real; that we may be clear of the awful guilt of using the name of Christ, and the mysteries of His Gospel, as mere matters of professional routine; or by a still more subtle delusion of the enemy, as instruments for obtaining for ourselves power over the minds of other men; but that we may indeed desire and advance their salvation. And without the reality of personal religion in ourselves, how can we hope to do any thing effectual for them? A bad man cannot be a good minister of Christ to others. They soon see through any unreality in us; they feel it in the pithless sermons, the dull moralities, or the mere sapless statements of doctrine without the life of personal experience, in which it vents itself.... They feel in one word that we are becoming the vendors of a charm, instead of being prophets with a message." *O si sic omnia!*

Before very long, however, although the Bishop continued to insist in his Sermons and Charges on the great realities of the Christian ministry, other dispositions manifested themselves.

Not many years after the secession of Mr. Newman, the Romanizing movement which he had originated assumed a new phase. Attempts were made to bring the Church of England to Rome by the furtive introduction not, as was Mr. Newman's method, of Romish doctrine, so much as of Romish practices and observances; and so the gradual accustoming of the public mind, especially in the case of the young, to the externals of the Romish system, in the hope that the doctrine would then follow of itself.

And of this movement it soon became apparent, both to friends and foes, that the Diocese of Oxford was the centre; 'the one above all others', as was observed by a writer[a] of the party, 'in which the externals of religion were cared for;' petty Romish peculiarities cropped up at Cuddesdon itself; and in other parishes, so says the same writer, 'altars, super-altars, credence-tables, sedilia, frontals, super-frontals, corporals, crosses, candles, &c. spoken of both by priests and people not as matters contested for, but as the natural parts of a well-built and well-ordered Church; Gregorian music, real or mutilated, having become the common use, and processions and processional crosses things not unheard of.' The opponents of the movement maintained, that 'in consequence[b] of the offensive

[a] Union Newspaper. The newspapers in the interest of the Romanizing party have been thus described by a member of the party:

"The Union, as every one knows, is a sort of vanguard in the army of the Church, and often comes in for sharp work, offensive and defensive too. The Guardian, with its broad sheet, 'safe' principles, and established position, is something like a main body to the Churchman's literary forces. Dr. Burgess brings up the rear with his Clerical Journal; and our venerable friend, the English Churchman, follows at an easy pace with the old women and the baggage."

The English Churchman (now defunct) was conducted with less ability than the Union, but was, if possible, still more bitter. Fuller, the Church historian, remarks, that "any man may be witty in a biting way; and those that have the dullest brains have commonly the sharpest teeth to that purpose."

[b] Thoughts on Church Matters in the Diocese of Oxford, by a Layman and Magistrate for that County.

accumulation on all sides of such innovating observances and practices, all belonging to the same class of religious views, and symptomatic of the same unprotestant tendency,' there was a 'widening breach between the Clergy and the Laity;' that 'numbers of the Clergy were filled with apprehension and mistrust, the Laity suspicious, dissatisfied, and alienated; and that, in spite of the many useful and popular qualities of the Bishop, attachment to the Church, and confidence in its ministers, was daily losing ground in the Diocese under his presidency[c].'

Still the Bishop was strong in his denunciations of direct Romish teaching.

The Rev. Temple West, Curate of Boyne-hill Church, was charged by a neighbouring Clergyman with putting improper questions to a sick woman, with the view of leading her to make confession to him. The Bishop issued a Commission to inquire into the charge, and the offence was not proved. He took advantage, however, of the occasion to make known to the public his sentiments respecting the Confessional in the following letter:

"*Lavington House, Petworth,*
Sept. 30.

"Gentlemen, I have received the report of your Commission of Inquiry into the charges brought

[c] Some Remarks upon the Visitation of Cuddesdon College, &c. by the Rev. R. Twopeny, B.D.

against Mr. West, and heartily accept as my own the decision at which, after a full examination of the matter, you have arrived.

"In thus formally adopting your decision, I wish, for the sake of my Diocese at large, to add a few words on the general subject of Confession.

"As I have already stated in writing to Mr. Shaw, I hold it to be a part of the wisdom and tenderness of the Church of England, that she provides for any parishioner who in sickness shall 'feel his conscience troubled with any weighty matter,' being 'moved to make special confession of his sins;' and that she also provides for those who, before Holy Communion, 'cannot quiet their own consciences,' being invited to 'open their grief to the minister of God's Word.'

"In mentioning this special and limited provision for troubled souls, I HOLD THAT THE CHURCH OF ENGLAND DISCOUNTENANCES ANY ATTEMPT ON THE PART OF HER CLERGY TO INTRODUCE A SYSTEM OF HABITUAL CONFESSION; or, in order to carry out such a system, to require men and women to submit themselves to the questioning and examination of the priest. Such a system of inquiry into the secrets of hearts must, in my judgment, lead to innumerable evils. GOD FORBID THAT OUR CLERGY SHOULD ADMINISTER, OR THAT OUR WIVES AND DAUGHTERS SHOULD BE SUBJECTED TO IT! I am sure that any attempt to introduce it would throw grievous difficulties in the way of that free ministerial intercourse with our people, which, for their sakes and for the efficiency of our ministry, it is all-important to maintain open and unsuspected.

"I am, &c.
"S. Oxon."

"*The Commissioners of the Boyne-hill Inquiry.*"

The circulation of a little work in the parish of St. Giles', Reading, which had been complained of by some of the parishioners, furnished the Bishop with an occasion, which he did not fail to avail himself of, of expressing equally Protestant sentiments on another important point; viz. the nature of our Lord's presence in the Sacrament of the Lord's Supper.

"*Whitchurch, near Reading, Nov.* 4, 1858.

"On the particular question as to which you have addressed me, nothing can be clearer than the declarations of our great Reformers, as they are embodied in our formularies. They maintain beyond all controversy the doctrine of our Lord's spiritual presence in His holy Sacrament; they utterly deny any change whatever of substance in the consecrated bread and wine, or any corporal or local[d] presence as accompanying the elements.

[d] If the Bishop has not altered his views, and the writer is not aware that he has, he cannot approve of the change of the words in 'the Christian Year'; "in the heart, not in the hands."

This plain statement of this great truth I thank God I altogether receive, and hold, and enforce, without equivocation or subterfuge, and *from* it I would not consent that there should be taken, nor *to* it added, one iota." *Letter to Dr. Cowan.*

The Bishop, however, still continuing to manifest a predilection for the externals of Romanism, the general distrust continued. Three occasions in particular served to call it out:

I. The Cuddesdon[e] College Inquiry.

II. The publication of a pamphlet, entitled, 'Facts and Documents, shewing the Alarming State of the Diocese.'

III. A Public Meeting held in the Theatre at Oxford in behalf of the St. Nicholas Middle Schools.

Each of these deserves special examination, as illustrative of the 'Position of the Bishop in reference to Ritualism.'

A separate consideration will also be given to certain features of his last few months' Episcopate, and particularly of his Charge delivered in December 1866.

[e] To be strictly accurate, it should be observed that the occurrences at Boyne-hill and Reading were preceded by the Cuddesdon College Inquiry.

To begin with

I. THE INQUIRY RESPECTING CUDDESDON THEOLOGICAL COLLEGE.

The College, which was founded in 1854, is by the first of its rules 'under the immediate direction of the Bishop of Oxford;' and, according to the Bishop's own statement, *'has not for its object to foster any party spirit,* but to nourish in young men going into Orders habits of self-denial, and true earnest piety, *on the simplest Church of England model.'*

Reports, however, emanating from the students of the College themselves, soon began to circulate in the Diocese, to the effect that, if the public were aware of certain features of the system pursued there, they would be greatly surprised and alarmed.

These reports gathered strength from an article in the Quarterly Review (Jan. 1858), from which the following is an extract:

"That theological Colleges should become the established door of entrance to the Ministry, would be the most disastrous blow the Church of England could receive. Those few which now exist, and which we must receive as established facts, may doubtless serve to meet the exceptional cases to which we have referred; but in order to make them as useful as they ought to be, the utmost vigilance on the part of their superiors is necessary to correct their inherent tendency to extravagance, and to obtain the confidence of the public by the most rigid forbearance from all sectarian teaching, and all external badges of party. If, instead of this indispensable neutrality of character, the visitor finds the Chapel fitted up with every fantastic decoration to which a party-meaning has been assigned; if he sees the altar adorned with flowers, surmounted with lights, covered with a lace-bordered napkin, and in every particular affecting the closest approximation to a popish model; if the Service of the Sacrament is attended with rites unsanctioned by any Rubric, with rinsings of cups in the newly-revived piscina, with genuflections and other ceremonial acts, which are foreign to our Ritual and usages; if in addition to all this he finds a Service-book in the Chapel, concocted from the seven canonical hours of the Romish Church, 'with additions and variations;' and if the servant, when applied to for an explanation, not familiar with the new nomenclature, stammers in hopeless confusion between sext and nones, primes and complines; what effect must this ostentatious playing at Romanism have on the Protestant public?

"It is not against this fantastic Ritual, as such, that we are now arguing. On this subject we have recently expressed our opinions at some length. We are remonstrating against the imprudence of thus trifling with the feeling of the country, and against the impropriety of conducting a place of public education in such an exclusive partisan spirit. If the pupil does not sympathize with what he sees and hears, the benefits which he might derive from the course of instruction are marred; if he does, his chance of usefulness and happiness in his future cure is compromised.

"It would be more agreeable to us to let this pass as a hypothetical case, perhaps as a rhetorical exaggeration. But, in so important a matter, to be plain spoken is a Christian duty, and our plainness, we hope, will give no offence to those of whose good intentions we are well assured. The College we allude to is Cuddesdon.

"This school of clerical training is supported by no endowment; but as a residence there is accepted by some of the Bishops, (as the prospectus informs us,) as a substitute for other conditions, which they had thought fit to impose on candidates for Holy Orders, we are justified in treating it as a public institution. Indeed the humblest place of education is a matter of public concern; and if the College of Cuddesdon is to enjoy the high privilege thus announced, it is a matter of moment that it should enjoy the public confidence. That confidence can never be bestowed on any institution for the training of youth—least of all the Clergy — which does not in its discipline and teaching, and in all its outward and visible arrangements, give ample guarantee that the principles of the Reformation, and the Ritual of the Church, are not held to be open questions."

A circular, calling attention to the foregoing extract from the Quarterly, having been sent to all the Clergy of the Diocese, the Bishop thought it desirable to appoint a Commission, consisting of the three Archdeacons, to examine into the state of the College. Their report contained the following admissions:

1. The Chapel was lavishly adorned with painting and gilding, and hangings at the east end, in a manner which the Commissioners considered highly objectionable.

2. The communion table had a raised shelf, the Roman predella.

3. There had formerly been a metal cross on this shelf.

4. There were darker coverings provided for the table in Advent and Lent, in accordance with the Rubric of the Roman Missal; and there had been upon it,

5. A cloth with lace, removed in consequence of the judgment of the Privy Council.

6. A piscina had been constructed in the Chapel, for which, according to our Ritual, there is no place or propriety.

7. The sacramental vessels had been rinsed in this piscina, according to the usage prevalent before the Reformation, but now discarded.

8. A Service-book was in use, entitled, 'Hours of Prayer,' which, 'though not containing or suggesting any doctrine at variance with that of the

Church of England' in the judgment of the Archdeacons, was 'cast in a form which bore an unfortunate resemblance to the Breviary of the Church of Rome.'

The report of the Archdeacons, though containing these admissions, was treated by the Bishop, in a published letter addressed to the Principal, probably to the no little surprise of the Archdeacons themselves, as ' COMPLETELY NEGATIVING EVERY CHARGE' BROUGHT AGAINST THE COLLEGE!! In spite of this, however, he proceeded to make considerable alterations, for which he was thus severely rated[f] in the Union, the then organ of

[f] Probably, not even in the days of Martin Mar-Prelate did there exist a party in the Church which has treated the Bishops, both individually and collectively, with the daring insolence of the Ritualistic writers. Even as long ago as the year 1838, in Froude's Remains, edited by Mr. Newman and Mr. Keble, there occurs the following passage : ' Nothing yet is so painful as *the defection of the Heads of the Church.* I hear that the Bishop of Ferns is dying; spes ultima.' Dr. Pusey has in general been more moderate, and was even charged by Sidney Smith with making 'oriental prostrations' to the Bishops. But he has long been free from any such infirmity. He used to say, that ' a Bishop's lightest word is heavy;' but by reprinting Tract XC, condemned by nearly the entire Episcopal body, he has shewn that he holds the collective authority of the Bishops very light. The later writers of the party are outrageous. Such expressions as 'the leaden mind of the Bishop of Chichester,' 'the callous tyranny of the Bishop of Manchester,' are familiar to the readers of the Church Times. A Fellow of University College, (Mr. Medd,)

the Ritualistic, or, as some would express it, the ultra-Ritualistic party:

"Having the opportunity of knowing the fact, we here plainly state it for the information of our readers in general, that the Bishop of Oxford is doing as much as possible to carry out those suggestions for Protestantizing Cuddesdon College, which have been made so frequently by various Puritan parsons. We are informed on the very best authority, viz. a Rector of high position in the immediate neighbourhood, that no less than twelve distinct concessions have from time to time been

in 'the Church and the World,' coolly says of the Bishop of Ely, that he is "one among the few members of the Episcopal bench who enjoy any reputation for theological acquirement;" and another writer in the same work, (Mr. Baring Gould,) that "the Episcopal boot is so accustomed to descend on every spark of vitality in the stubble of the Establishment, that perhaps it will follow the precedent—the illustrious precedent of the Wesleyan schism—and stamp out all this zeal (i.e. that of the Romanizing party) for God and His Church." The British Critic, (July 1866,) writing in the same strain, thus woos the Bishop of Oxford: "Whereas the Church party had elevated the Bishops to the highest pinnacle of influence in 1844, the opinion of a Bishop passes for nothing now, unless it be in itself wise and prudent. It is much to the regretted, no doubt, but it is an undoubted fact, that the Bishops have lost an immense amount of influence—an influence which we gladly admit will be *most easily regained by any Bishop who will throw himself heartily into the Catholic movement of the day.*"

made; the list of which has been forwarded to us for insertion; viz.

1. Removal of the altar-cross.

2. Discountenance of the change of altar-frontals.

3. The blotting out the figures of the Saints and Apostles, which stood at the East end of the Chapel, being the work of a then resident student.

4. The removal of a beautifully painted reredos, designed by Mr. Street.

5. The removal of the silken hangings.

6. The disuse of flowers on the ledge behind the altar.

7. The disuse of the piscina.

8. The disuse of two lights at the time of communion.

9. The disuse of the 'Book of Prayer.'

10. The discountenance of three services out of five, which were formerly said daily.

11. THE DISCOUNTENANCE OF PRIVATE CONFESSION.

12. The dismissal of the College authorities."

The writer then went on to remark in a strain of bitter sarcasm, that the Bishop had 'met the most reasonable and modest demands made upon him, with a consideration and courtesy which was beyond all praise.' Every thing objected to had been promptly removed, and now the Chapel was duly prepared for that 'sober, solemn, and expressive Ritual,' of which the Bishop approved. 'One half-gallon of whitewash judiciously applied, and the sanctuary might, perhaps, present an appearance even still more in accordance with the customary simplicity of our beloved Church.'

A subsequent N°. of the Union contained the following Jeremiad, headed, CUDDESDON AS IT WAS, AND AS IT IS:

"In a few weeks, if report speaks true, there will be a grand demonstration at Cuddesdon College. The annual festival would be agreeable enough to read about or join in, did we not know, from authentic sources, that the changes which were made by the Bishop, at the suggestion of the Quarterly Review, have in all truth and sobriety utterly ruined the College[f]. Now it is no longer what it was in its early and palmy days. The immense success which it obtained, the real earnest work which was effected there, is reversed altogether. An atmosphere of respectability exists around and about; and, in too many cases, successful attempts are made wholly and utterly to blot out the bright remembrances and good traditions of a better and more Catholic *régime*. Frequent celebrations—if we are not mis-

[f] Here and there there have been omitted some offensive expressions in reference to the Bishop and Archdeacons, in accordance with George Herbert's rule:
"He pares his apple, who would cleanly feed."

C

informed—are no more, being possibly regarded as 'a corrupt following of the Apostles;' private confession is altogether discountenanced, and fasting before Holy Communion is calmly characterized as 'a mediæval folly,' or a 'servile imitation of a most corrupt form of Christianity.' Cranmer, of all things under the sun, is spoken of as 'a martyr' (!); and many earnest warnings are given against any dangerous deviations from a firm holding *to the blasphemous formulas of the heresiarch Luther on Justification.* In fact, little remains the same, as of old, but the building; and one most happy change has been gradually effected. Of old there were always more than *twenty students;* now (after every attempt to hook them in has been made and failed) there are but *seven!* And the truth is, that the polite dismissal of the very man, Mr. Liddon, who stamped an impress upon Cuddesdon College and made it a success, has turned out a more fatal mistake and a greater loss than was ever anticipated. Many enrolled themselves as *alumni* for the single and simple privilege of sitting at his feet; for he is verily a Tractarian 'Gamaliel.' This the Bishop of Oxford might have known by inquiry, and possibly did know when he sent him adrift. His successor is—but we wont draw comparisons, for they are odious—well, his successor is very unlike him, as the result alluded to above implies."

Mr. Liddon's successor, the late lamented Mr.

Swinny, was a Protestant, and a good and pious man. It is to be hoped that the improvements which he effected still continue now that the College has passed into other hands.

It is time to pass on to another topic, viz.

II. THE PUBLICATION OF THE PAMPHLET, ENTITLED, 'FACTS AND DOCUMENTS, SHEWING THE ALARMING STATE OF THE DIOCESE OF OXFORD.'

This pamphlet was published early in the year 1859. The grounds of the writer's alarm were the introduction, actual or attempted, into the Diocese of fifteen Romish peculiarities; viz.

1. Auricular Confession.
2. Altar crosses and crucifixes.
3. Processions, and processional crosses and banners.
4. Stone altars.
5. The Romish wafer.
6. Mixing water with wine at the Eucharist.
7. Elevation of the elements.
8. Bowing to the elements.
9. The priest crossing himself.
10. Anointing of the sick.
11. Prayers for the dead.
12. Masses for the dead.
13. Romish vestments.
14. Romish ornaments.
15. Sisterhoods.

The writer, after referring to the Cuddesdon College inquiry, and certain proceedings in a parish in Sussex, of which the Bishop of Oxford was the patron, concluded with some remarks upon the position of the Bishop; and was greatly blamed by some for referring to the secession to Rome of several members of his Lordship's family, of whom the most distinguished was his brother-in-law, Archdeacon Manning, now calling himself Archbishop of Westminster. It was indeed a delicate subject, but if he thought it necessary to consider the position of the Bishop at all, this was too important a feature of it to be passed over in silence.

The pamphlet was forwarded to the Clergy and to many of the Laity of the Diocese, and the effects anticipated were so serious, that the three Archdeacons, together with twenty-four of the Rural Deans, came forward, and presented to the Bishop the following Address:

" My Lord,

" We, the undersigned, (being Archdeacons and Rural Deans in the Diocese,) address your Lordship under most unusual circumstances.

" It has come to our knowledge that a pamphlet, entitled, *Facts and Documents, shewing the Alarming State of the Diocese of Oxford,* has been sent round to the Churchwardens and other laymen of the Diocese. We have felt bound carefully to examine the statements made in it; and having done so, and thinking it possible that, professing to come from 'A Senior Clergyman of the Diocese,' they may be believed by some who have not an opportunity of ascertaining the facts of the case, and so produce unquietness and disaffection, we feel further bound to declare, from our own knowledge of the Diocese, that they are unjustifiable misrepresentations. The writer states that the Diocese of Oxford is the centre of a Romanizing movement, and he grounds this charge on the publication by a Mr. Purchas, of the University of Cambridge, of a book called *Directorium Anglicanum,* revised by an Incumbent of this Diocese; and of an anonymous work called, *The Churchman's Diary;* and on no better foundation than the publication of these two books, the writer proceeds to the charge of the introduction of fifteen peculiarities of the Romish system; and, further, he insinuates that this attempt has received your sanction.

"Now we, who are well acquainted with the actual state of this Diocese, hereby solemnly declare to your Lordship, that, to the best of our knowledge and belief, this charge is absolutely false and calumnious,—that there is nothing whatever introduced, or attempted to be introduced, among us to justify the assertion that the Diocese is in an alarming state, or that your Lordship has ever sanctioned any peculiarities of the Romish system. We should, as earnestly as any could, contend against the introduction of such peculiarities. We conceive, from the extracts we have seen from it, that Mr. Purchas's book is a very unwise and mischievous publication. We are strongly opposed to all attempts to alter in any respects the Ritual of our Reformed Church, of which we are, as our fathers were before us, loyal and affectionate sons. We are confident, from our experience of your Episcopal rule of fourteen years among us, that these are also your convictions and principles of action; and many of us know instances in which, where young and inexperienced men have been led in this direction, you have kindly but firmly restrained them, and corrected their errors. We therefore feel bound solemnly to declare that the statements of the 'Senior Clergyman' are, in our judgment, presumptuous and unfounded calumnies against your Lordship in this Diocese.

  Charles C. Clerke, Archdeacon of Oxford.
  E. Bickersteth, Archdeacon of Bucks.
  J. Randall, Archdeacon of Berks.
    &c. &c."

 This declaration of the Archdeacons and Rural Deans (six of the latter body however having refused to subscribe it) had a very important effect. It elicited from the Bishop some very Protestant sentiments, and a protest from not less than one hundred of the Clergy against the Romanizing innovations.

The following are extracts from the Bishop's reply :

"Rev. and Dear Brethren,

"You have well exposed the frivolous grounds on which this scandal has been founded. Our Diocese has no peculiar share in that sad list of apostates[g] to the Papacy, which has been culled from all the Dioceses of England for many years past; neither has it any connection with the book of Mr. Purchas; and the attempt to connect us with it, because one clergyman who holds preferment, and another who was once a student within our borders, are said to have revised its sheets, is transparently futile. So far as I know, there is not one[h] clergyman in the Diocese who has been so weak as to attempt practically to introduce into his parish the ritualistic system of the writer. For myself, I rejoice in the opportunity which your Address gives of declaring thus publicly that, with you, I UTTERLY DISAPPROVE ALL ATTEMPTS TO INTRODUCE ANY SUCH UNUSUAL RITUALISTIC DEVELOPEMENTS. I DEEM IT UNPARDONABLE THAT WE, WHO ARE CHARGED

[g] The Bishop forgets for the moment that Mr. Newman, the most distinguished of these, had been Vicar of St. Mary's in Oxford.

[h] There are now six, if not seven, churches in Oxford itself in the hands of the ritualistic party. One of the Incumbents has gone beyond Mr. Purchas, for he substituted on Good Friday 1866 a Romish Service, the Improperia or Reproaches, for that of the Afternoon Service of the Church of England.

WITH THE ALL-IMPORTANT WORK OF SEEKING TO WIN SOULS FOR WHICH CHRIST DIED, SHOULD WASTE OUR OWN ENERGIES, AND ESTRANGE THE HEARTS OF OUR PEOPLE, BY GIVING OURSELVES UP TO SUCH CHILDISH FRIVOLITIES.

"I know well that unwearied and reiterated misrepresentations have led many who have viewed me from afar to suppose that I am favourable to these innovations. But you know me better; you know that I could point to all the high diocesan offices, and to every important parish I have had to fill, and could shew that I have placed in them hearty English Churchmen, free from all extremes either of doctrine or ritual. You know that I HOLD IT TO BE MY DUTY TO MAINTAIN FIRMLY, AND WITHOUT COMPROMISE, (though with the utmost charity in judgment, word, and conduct to those who differ from us,) THE DISTINCTIVE DOCTRINES OF OUR OWN REFORMED CHURCH, AND THE SOLEMN AND EXPRESSIVE RITUAL WHICH IS SO CLOSELY CONNECTED WITH THEM. YOU KNOW THAT TO THE UTMOST OF MY POWER I DISCOURAGE ALL DIMINUTION, AND ALL EXCESS OF HER SOBER RULE. YOU WELL KNOW THAT I HAVE A JEALOUS DREAD OF EVERY ROMANIZING TENDENCY, AND THAT I HAVE NOT THE SLIGHTEST SYMPATHY WITH THOSE WHO WISH TO RESTORE AMONG US SUCH A RITUAL AS MR. PURCHAS DESCRIBES,—FOR THAT, IN MY OPINION, SUCH ATTEMPTS BOTH BREED ON THE ONE SIDE, IN SOME WEAK MINDS, A LONGING FIRST FOR THE GORGEOUS RITUAL, AND THEN FOR THE

CORRUPT DOCTRINES OF ROME; AND ON THE OTHER, TEND FAR MORE WIDELY TO ALIENATE OUR PEOPLE FROM SOUND CHURCH OF ENGLAND PRINCIPLES, AND GIVE OCCASION TO SUCH CALUMNIES AS THOSE WHICH YOU HAVE CONDEMNED."

So strong a denunciation of Ritualism of course drew down upon the Bishop fresh sneers from the Union. The meaning of Protestants, who condemned Catholic practices, was plain enough; but "it would puzzle Solomon himself to understand the policy of the Bishop[i], and those who addressed him so recently. Quietly and 'on the sly,' (as it were,) Catholic practices are not only permitted, but approved; but, as soon as public opinion is

---

[i] The following is an extract from a letter of Father Philip, the Queen's Confessor, to Cardinal Barberini, in the days of Archbishop Laud:
"Those who were most favourably inclined to the Catholic cause were frequently obliged to give proofs of their zeal to the contrary for fear of notice, *in which case it was difficult to form a just idea of their real sentiments*, seeing they found themselves under a necessity of varying from themselves and acting incoherently." After stating that this remark applied to the Bishops in particular, "though several of them were disposed to enter into a correspondence with Rome," Father Philip goes on to say, that "such a conduct as this had so much of contradiction in it, that it was altogether unintelligible to those who were not perfectly acquainted with the infirmities of human nature, and particularly with the irresolution of these islanders." Panzani's Memoirs, pp. 186, 187. See Dean Goode's Rome's Tactics, pp. 30, 31.

aroused, principles are flung to the winds : wordy addresses, or anti-Roman claptrap, are published, and some person or thing is readily sacrificed. It is a known fact, that the Bishop's sympathies have been and are with the Catholic party in the English Church. And, appreciating his great ability, we rejoice that it is so. Our only regret is, that he has not the moral courage to say so. If he had, and boldly took his stand upon some definite and palpable principle, he would be far more respected than he is. But *it is evident, that our opponents are sharp enough to perceive that his occasional abuse of Popery, and condemnations of the 'gorgeous Ritual' and 'corrupt doctrines of Rome,' will not serve to balance his judicious appreciation of the truths of Catholicity, and of those Clergymen of his Diocese who so admirably proclaim them. 'Res non verba' is their motto, and an admirable sentiment it is; and so by consequence they are on the look-out for what is done rather than what is said.*"

That there was some truth in the concluding sentences of the above extract from the Union, will appear by the following

Remonstrance,

Addressed by One Hundred of the Clergy of the Diocese to the Archdeacons and Rural Deans.

"We, the undersigned Clergy of the three Archdeaconries of Oxford, have read with surprise and deep regret an Address to the Lord Bishop of the Diocese, signed by all the three Archdeacons and twenty-four of the Rural Deans; and we feel painfully necessitated, under the peculiar circumstances of the case, to present to the Clergy and Laity throughout the Diocese a counter-statement to what is therein asserted, which we do in the form of an Address to the parties signing. In doing so, we wholly abstain from expressing any opinion upon the anonymous pamphlet, *Facts and Documents*, &c. to which the Address refers; and we declare that we have no wish to provoke strife or controversy, nor do we entertain the slightest feeling of ill-will towards the respected parties who have been led to subscribe their names to the Address. On the contrary, we have a sanguine hope that this movement will lead to the future peace of the Diocese. Our object is to uphold, by God's help, that pure Reformed Religion which we have received from our forefathers, and which is the glory of our Church.

"Venerable and Reverend Sirs,

"You have all of you assured our Bishop that you 'have felt bound carefully to examine the statements made in the Facts and Documents,' that you are 'well acquainted with the actual state of this Diocese,' and you feel bound to declare, from your own knowledge of the Diocese, that the statements are 'unjustifiable misrepresentations.' And again, you 'feel bound solemnly to declare that the statements of the Senior Clergyman are in your judgment presumptuous and unfounded calumnies against the Bishop in this Diocese.'

"To this the Bishop, as might be reasonably expected, replies, 'You are the best possible witnesses as to their truth or falsehood; living, as you do, in every part of the three counties, &c. the facts of the case must be known to you, while your high character makes your testimony concerning them unimpeachable.'

"Now we have too good reason to call in question the decision to which you have come; and whilst we think it probable that the haste, with which your Address appears to have been prepared and sent round for signatures, had led to some of you having affixed your names without sufficient inquiry, we feel it to be our very painful duty to bring matters to an issue, that the Church at large may know the truth and judge accordingly. We therefore, with all respect, appeal

"(1) To the Venerable the Archdeacon of Oxford, and the Rev. the Rural Dean of Oxford, to say whether there are not (as asserted in Facts and Documents, p. 15) stone-altars in the following Churches and Chapels in your Archdeaconry and Rural Deanery, and within a walk or ride of your residences; 1. St. Thomas in Oxford, 2. Binsey, 3. Wolvercote, 4. Littlemore, 5. Sandford, 6. St.

John's, 7. 8. 9. the three Cemetery Chapels in Oxford?

"Further, we appeal to you to say whether, at least since the judgment of the Judicial Committee of the Privy Council, it is not actually unlawful to have stone-altars in Churches; and whether, with the following sentence of that judgment before you, you are prepared 'to contend, as earnestly as any can, against' this 'peculiarity of the Romish system.'

"' *The distinction between an altar and a communion table is in itself essential, and deeply founded in the most important difference in matters of faith between Protestants and Roman Catholics; viz. in the different notions of the nature of the Lord's Supper which prevailed in the Roman Catholic Church at the time of the Reformation, and those which were introduced by the Reformers.*'

"(2) We appeal again to the Venerable the Archdeacon of Oxford, and the Rev. the Rural Dean of Cuddesdon, the latter till very lately Principal of Cuddesdon College, the former appointed by the Bishop to inquire into the state of the College, to say whether the enumeration of the practices which have at one time or other prevailed in the College Chapel, (Facts and Documents, pp. 30, 31,) is a 'presumptuous and unfounded calumny,' or correct; and whether these are not of 'Romish tendency?' They are as follows:

"1. The Chapel lavishly adorned with painting

and gilding, and hangings at the east end, in a manner which the visitors thought objectionable.

" 2. An altar shelf, or super-altar.

" 3. A metal cross formerly on this shelf.

" 4. Darker coverings on the table during Advent and Lent, in accordance with the Rubric of the Roman Missal.

" 5. A cloth with lace, now discontinued in consequence of the judgment of the Privy Council.

" 6. A piscina constructed in the Chapel, for which, according to our Ritual, there is no place or propriety.

" 7. The Sacramental vessels rinsed in this piscina, according to the usage prevalent before the Reformation, but now discarded.

" 8. A Service-book, entitled, ' Hours of Prayer,' bearing an unfortunate resemblance to the Breviary of the Roman Church; with the title of Antiphons, and the obsolete designation of Hours.

"We also ask whether it is a 'presumptuous and unfounded calumny,' or the truth, that subsequently to the inquiry three students (p. 31) 'have joined the Church of Rome;' and whether another student is not entirely identified with the ' Directorium Anglicanum,' (which you consider 'a mischievous publication,') inasmuch as he is called by Mr. Purchas his ' fellow-labourer and joint-compiler ?'

" (3) We next beg leave to appeal to the Venerable the Archdeacon of Berks. and the Rev. the Rural Dean of Abingdon, to say whether there is not a stone-altar in the Church of Radley, in their Archdeaconry and Rural Deanery?

"(4) And to the same Venerable Archdeacon, and the Rural Dean of Wantage, to say whether there is not a stone-altar, i.e. a stone-slab, supported by blocks of wood, in the parish Church of Wantage, set up within these last few years through the instrumentality of the Rural Dean himself; and we appeal to the Archdeacon and the two Rural Deans, after reference to the sentence of the Judicial Committee of the Privy Council, quoted and referred to above, to say whether these are not contrary to law, and 'peculiarities of the Romish system?'

"(5) We appeal to the Archdeacon of Buckingham, and the two Rural Deans of Mursley, (1st and 2nd Portions,) to say whether the brief account of the procession at Addington, with processional crosses and banners, given at p. 14 of 'Facts and Documents,' is an 'unjustifiable misrepresentation,' or the truth?

"(6) We also ask the Rural Deans of Cuddesdon and Wallingford to state, whether the following sentence (pp. 13, 14 of Facts and Documents) is, or is not a 'calumny?' 'A procession with processional crosses took place at the Anniversary of Cuddesdon College in 1855, and was so strongly objected to by some of the Clergy, that the Bishop promised that it should not occur again.'

"We might proceed further in these inquiries,

but having stated matters which cannot be proved to be 'misrepresentations,' we think it sufficient to call on all and each of the Archdeacons and Rural Deans who have signed this Address, 'and examined the statements, and are well acquainted with this Diocese,' to specify one by one what are the statements which they feel bound solemnly to declare are 'unjustifiable misrepresentations,' and 'presumptuous and unfounded calumnies.' We ask this not with the view of justifying or defending the 'Senior Clergyman of the Diocese;' but because we are fully persuaded that the more searching the inquiry which is made into the state of things in this Diocese, the more will all rightminded men, instead of allowing themselves to believe that there is 'nothing whatever introduced or attempted to be introduced among us to justify the assertion that the Diocese is in an alarming state,' see that there is good cause for alarm and anxiety; and that the unquietness and disaffection which the Archdeacons and Rural Deans think likely to be produced, are not owing to the publication of *Facts and Documents,* but to the facts and documents themselves, both those brought to light in this and other pamphlets, and those facts which are known in their several neighbourhoods.

"We now venture to express our earnest hope that our brethren who have signed this Address will feel encouraged, by the assurance given to them by the Bishop that he has 'a jealous dread of every Romanizing tendency,' to use their influence, and whatever authority they have in their own spheres, that not merely the things specified in this statement, but every thing else which in any measure savours of Romanism, and is a departure from the spirit of the Reformed and Protestant Church of England, may be abandoned, that so all the causes of distrust may cease, and peace be restored.

(Signed)
    E. A. Litton, Rector of St. Clement's, Oxford.
    H. W. Lloyd, Vicar of Cholsey.
    W. R. Fremantle, Vicar of Claydon, Bucks.
    J. Tucker, Vicar of West Hendred.
    R. Twopeny, Vicar of North Stoke with Ipsden.
    Wriothesley Russell, Rector of Chenies, and Canon of Windsor.
    A. Musgrave, Rector of Chinnor and Emmington.
    Septimus Cotes, Rector of Newington.
    Samuel Whittingham, Rector of Childrey.
    J. Flory Howard, Rector of Yattendon.
    J. Langley, Rector of St. Mary's, Wallingford.
    H. Barne, Vicar of Faringdon.
    Edmund Thompson, Curate of Faringdon.
    W. J. A. Langford, Vicar of Watlington.
    J. Prosser, Vicar of Thame.
    J. W. Peers, Vicar of Tetsworth.
    J. W. Watts, Vicar of Bicester.

H. D. Harington, Vicar of South Newington.
J. R. Hughes, Rector of Newnton Longville.
Arthur Isham, Rector of Weston Turville.
Herbert White, Incumbent of Warborough.
J. M. Butt, Vicar of Wingrave.
John Shaw, Vicar of Stoke Poges.
James Niven, Vicar of Swanbourne.
W. W. McCreight, Vicar of Winslow.
Joshua Greaves, Vicar of Great Missenden.
F. W. Young, Curate of Great Missenden.
W. J. Marshall, Rector of Grendon Underwood.
H. Paddon, Vicar of High Wycombe.
Alfred M. Preston, Curate of East Claydon.
R. Bennett Burges, Curate of Steeple Claydon.
G. I. Tubbs, Incumbent of St. Mary's, Reading.
W. W. Phelps, Incumbent of Trinity, Reading.
J. Ball, Vicar of St. Lawrence, Reading.
J. R. Burgess, Vicar of Streatley.
J. Gore, Vicar of Shalbourne.
E. Stanley James, Vicar of Letcombe Regis.
James Hearn, Rector of Hatford.
G. Valpy, Vicar of Bucklebury.
F. G. Lemann, Vicar of Langford.
J. Browne, Curate of Halton.
W. W. Walton, Curate of Waddesdon.
W. J. Burgess, Incumbent of Lacy Green.
T. B. Holt, Vicar of Little Horwood.
E. L. Smith, Incumbent of Barton and Chetwode.
J. Harrison, Vicar of Dinton.
J. Smith Hill, Curate of Dinton.

W. E. Ward, Incumbent of Iver.
W. P. Perry, Incumbent of Chislehampton.
T. J. Lingwood, Curate of Bicester.
Joseph West, Incumbent of Holy Trinity, Oxford.
T. Curme, Vicar of Sandford.
E. W. Pulling, Chaplain of Littlemore Asylum.
Peter Maurice, Vicar of Yarnton.
W. Green, Vicar of Steeple Barton.
G. T. Cameron, Curate of St. Ebbe's, Oxford.
J. Jordan, Vicar of Enstone.
N. Denton, Curate of North Stoke.
Walter Gibbs, Incumbent of Tyler's Green.
D. Watkins, Vicar of Thornborough.
S. W. White, Curate of Winslow.
J. C. Addison, Incumbent of Wotton Underwood.
Frederick Young, Incumbent of Walton.
T. O. Hall, Curate of Penn.
Adam Baynes, Rector of Adstock.
C. F. Champneys, Vicar of Wendover.
J. Macdonald, Vicar of Blewbury.
Alfred Butler, Incumbent of Penn-Street.
Edward Geare, Curate of Woodstock.
W. H. Lloyd, Curate of Middle Claydon.
George Alford, Rector of Aston Sandford.
Henry Meeres, Vicar of Haddenham.
Richard Meredith, Vicar of Hagbourne.
Henry Linton, Rector of St. Peter-le-Bailey, Oxford.
J. G. Browne, Rector of Kiddington.
E. Ward Pears, Curate of Stoke Goldington.
W. E. Richardson, Incumbent of Linslade.

John Thornton, Vicar of Aston Abbots.
James Hazel, Incumbent of Nettlebed.
John Holding, Incumbent of Ashampstead.
S. W. Barnett, Vicar of Towersey.
W. H. Stokes, Vicar of Goring.
Arthur Hoskins, Curate of St. Peter-le-Bailey, Oxford.
Charles Blackman, Rector of Chesham Bois.
J. W. Deans, Vicar of Kintbury.
H. H. Phelps, Curate of Trinity, Reading.
E. Arnold, Incumbent of Loudwater.
John R. Rushton, Incumbent of Hooknorton.
Francis Pocock, Curate of Little Faringdon.
T. T. Churton, Rector of West Shefford.
W. S. Bricknell, Vicar of Eynsham.
T. C. Whitehead, Incumbent of Gawcott.
R. D. Rawnsley, Vicar of Shiplake.
W. Payne, Incumbent of St. John's, Reading.
F. B. Blenkin, Curate of St. John's, Reading.
H. S. M. Hubert, Rector of Marsh Baldon.
F. A. Dawson, Rector of Buscot.
J. Pavitt Penson, Vicar of Clanfield.
T. W. Cockell, Curate of Stanford-Dingley.
J. Thorpe, Chaplain of the County Prison."

The above manifesto, remarkable not only for its contents, but for the number and weight of the names attached to it, more particularly considering the known reluctance of the Clergy to take any public step in opposition to the wishes of their

Bishop, found its way into the Times. It was followed by 'a flight of pamphlets' marked by this happy peculiarity, that, whether siding with the author of 'Facts and Documents' or opposed to him, they were written in the style and spirit which elicited the well-known compliment of Bishop Tomline to Mr. Scott the commentator, addressed to his son, 'Sir, your father's answer to my book was that of a scholar, a christian, and a gentleman.'

A further step however was taken by the anti-ritualistic Clergy. Many of those who had *remonstrated* with the Archdeacons and Rural Deans thought it incumbent upon them to make known their sentiments to the Bishop himself, and did so in an Address, which elicited a further expression of opinion from his Lordship. He treated most of the things complained of as trifles, justified the use of the cross in our churches "*as distinct from the Romish superstitions of the crucifix,*" and excused super-altars or altar-shelves, and processions. On one point he no doubt felt great difficulty. In objecting to stone altars, which in many churches in the Diocese had been substituted for wooden communion tables, the Clergy had reminded him of the judgment of the Privy Council in 1857:

" The distinction between an altar and a communion table is in itself essential, and deeply founded in the most important difference in matters of faith between Protestants and Romanists; viz. in the different notions of the nature of the Lord's Supper which prevailed in the Roman Catholic Church at the time of the Reformation, and those which were intended by the Reformers." With reference to this very judgment, the Bishop had said, in his Charge delivered the same year, that its decisions were 'binding upon our consciences, as Clergy, by our oaths and promises at ordination, licensing, or institution;' and that it would be "*his own duty to ascertain,* previous to any future Visitation, *that its injunctions had been obeyed.*" But he took a different view of his duty now. "In answer to your urgent request, 'that stone altars may be removed,' I can only say that, as to any already existing, *you have the same power of removing them as I have;* nor, where they have long stood, are connected with no false doctrine or superstitious use, and where they cause no dissatisfaction to the parishioners, *do I think it wise to move* in the matter. But if you or any others think differently, the remedy is in your own hands; for they can be removed by a process in the Ecclesiastical Court, which it is in the power of the aggrieved parties to promote." In other words, the Bishop knew that the law was on the side of the complaining Clergy, but flatly refused to enforce it.

The Address of the Clergy was followed up by one to the same effect from four thousand of the Laity of the Diocese, among whom were "three

Members of Parliament, twenty-three Magistrates, and one hundred and seventy-nine Churchwardens, the remainder almost wholly consisting of Gentlemen, Farmers, and Tradesmen." But the reply of the Bishop throwing no fresh light upon his position in reference to Ritualism, it is time to pass on to

III. THE PUBLIC MEETING HELD IN THE SHELDONIAN THEATRE AT OXFORD IN BEHALF OF THE ST. NICHOLAS MIDDLE SCHOOLS.

The Meeting was a very important and influential one. Two Dukes who were expected (Newcastle and Marlborough) did not appear, but there were present the Bishops of Oxford, Chichester, and Rochester, the Chancellor of the Exchequer (Mr. Gladstone), and other distinguished persons from a distance, besides many Heads of Houses, and other leading Members of the University. The Schools for which the support of the Meeting was solicited were for the benefit of the Lower Middle Classes in connection with St. Nicholas College; a Society which, according to the terms of its Trust-deed, had for its object the promotion of education "in the doctrines and principles of the Church now established, as the same are set forth in the Book of Common Prayer, and administration of the Sacraments, and other rites and ceremonies of the said Church." The Vice-Chancellor, Dr. Jeune, now Bishop of Peterborough, took the chair.

A few hours, however, before the Meeting took place the following handbill had been widely circulated in the University:

"PUBLIC MEETING IN THE THEATRE.

"MIDDLE SCHOOLS

"In connection with St. Nicholas College, Lancing.

"The attention of Members of the University and others about to attend the above Meeting is called to the following facts:—

"1. Confession is encouraged among the boys at these Schools. Many influential Clergy in the neighbourhood withhold their support from the Schools on this account.

"2. Crucifixes are distributed among the boys on leaving the Schools.

"The following statement can be supported on oath:—

"'Some three years since a young friend of mine who was being educated at St. John's College, Hurstpierpoint, lodged in my house during an illness. He wore a crucifix, some four inches in length, made of silver, and suspended by a ribbon round his neck. He declared that he, in common with his companions, had it given him at the above-mentioned College.'"

This handbill was treated at the Meeting with utter contempt. The Bishop of Chichester pronounced its statements to be 'myths.' The

Vice-Chancellor 'did not believe that any English gentlemen, any English clergymen, would boldly propound to them a scheme, which, under the guise of loyal attachment to the Church of England, was designed to entrap them into promoting principles at variance with her principles, and the allegiance they owed to her.' The Bishop of Oxford expressed himself still more strongly. 'There was a serpent in Paradise, and we have found that there is a snake in the grass of Hurstpierpoint.' The 'snake in the grass' was the writer of the handbill, but it appeared that his Lordship was not without his apprehensions that there might be more than one snake. 'Assuming that there are SUCH INSIDIOUS ATTEMPTS and SUCH EVIL PRINCIPLES AT WORK,' (i.e. such *as distributing crucifixes among the boys* and *encouraging confession*,) 'how are they to be best counteracted?' Some might think that the best way would be to send the boys to another school. But the Bishop had a different method. 'How do you prevent one or two ill-conditioned fellows carrying out their own ill-conditioned schemes? Why, by filling the room with honest men. Then let the honest men in Oxford come forward with their love of truth, and their affection for our Protestant Church, and these suspected malignants, with their dark practices, will be foiled in their evil designs. It is the part of such a body as this to see that there is depth of principle, and honesty in carrying that principle out, in the educational labours carried on throughout the country.'

A few days after the Meeting the author of the handbill came forward, and in his own name addressed a public letter to the Vice-Chancellor. In proof of his assertion, that crucifixes had been distributed among the boys of Mr. Woodard's schools, he produced an affidavit sworn before a Brighton Magistrate, Sir George Westphal; and, in order to shew that confession was practised among them, a letter from Mr. Woodard himself to a Sussex Clergyman admitting the fact, and another letter addressed to Mr. Woodard by the Bishop of Chichester, which seems to imply that such confession was followed, after the Romish method, by penance and absolution. The Bishop thus expresses himself:

"*Wadhurst*, 10*th May*, 1851.

"My dear Mr. Woodard,—In the course of my Confirmation circuit I have heard occasionally of the Shoreham and Hurst Schools, and, I am sorry to say, always in a manner leading to the conclusion, that there is a grave and growing distrust as to the way in which the boys are led to make communications regarding their religious state. In two instances, as you are aware, pupils have been withdrawn on that ground.

"Now whatever Dr. Pusey or any other person may say, THERE CAN BE NO DOUBT THAT OUR

Anglican Church and system repudiate the private confessional; nor ought (or fairly can) the few words which occur in one of the Exhortations to the receiving of the Holy Communion to be perverted into the sanction of the general use, or of any thing approaching to a regular systematic employment, of the confessional. I must rely upon you for taking care that my views on this point are adopted by the officers of the institution, as those by which they are to regulate themselves. The boys should be taught to examine and to strive to frame their conduct upon religious principles; but their confessions should be made unto God, when they have weighed their sayings and doings by the rule of His Word and Commandments. And then repentance and sorrow for transgression should follow, and the offering of them as from a contrite heart. But no recourse should be had to self-inflicted or priest-enjoined penance, as a means or an instrument of obtaining pardon for sin. Our Church rejects such penances as these, and penance as in any way a sacrament. Experience justifies her; for experience shews that always these things, instead of enlightening, corrupt and weaken the conscience, and lead the individual to depend on some other weak and frail human being, instead of learning to see and scan himself in the pure mirror of God's Word, and to regulate himself by an informed and sensitive conscience of his own, seeking its guidance in the Word, and strengthened thereby.

"I should be very sorry that so noble an undertaking as yours should fail from any cause; but it will, and I MUST ADD IT OUGHT, IF CONFESSION, AND PENANCE, AND CONSEQUENT ABSOLUTION ARE INTRODUCED INTO IT. I hope then you will be vigilant on this point, and I must beg you to regard me as now writing Visitorially; wherefore I beg this may be communicated to all whom it concerns.

"Your faithful brother,
"A. T. CICESTR."
"*To the Rev. Mr. Woodard.*"

Further inquiry brought to light other Romanizing practices in these professedly Church of England places of education, as to which it appeared, from the published letter of a candidate for a vacant mastership, that the officials were *pledged to secrecy*!! Attention has been drawn of late[i] to the work of a Mr. Purchas, one of the extreme ritualistic writers, called the Directorium Anglicanum, the object of which work is to shew how much of the Romish system it is possible for a Clergyman to introduce into the

[i] See Quarterly Review, Jan. 1867, on Ultra-Ritualism. This article, together with the recently-published work of the Dean of Ripon 'Rome's Tactics,' and the Bishop of St. David's Charge, the ritualistic party ignore as much as possible.

Services of the Church of England, without rendering himself liable to a prosecution. The directions given therein, for the due performance of the Burial Service, will serve to throw light on the following narrative:

"On Wednesday last, the funeral of one of the boys of St. John's College, Hurstpierpoint, was carried out in a solemn and Christian manner. At a quarter past eight o'clock, a choral celebration (i.e. of the Sacrament of the Lord's Supper) took place in the temporary Chapel, the coffin being in the nave, below the chancel step, between the large wax tapers. The parish pall which covered the coffin had a white cross extending the whole length of it; and in the corners four red crosses. At the head of the coffin lay a bunch of autumn flowers. Upon each side of the altar stood a triangle of lighted candles. A second similar celebration was held at half-past ten o'clock; after which, having sung the Psalm *De profundis*[k], the procession formed, and left the Church, chanting the *Miserere mei*[k] to the third tone first ending, having an interval between each verse, while the Chapel bell tolled. Having wound round the cloisters, the choir, coffin, and mourners passed out of the College gate, followed by a long line of boys singing. On reaching the gate out of the

---

[k] The use of these Psalms, which form no part of the Burial Service of the Church of England, is prescribed by the Roman Ritual.

College grounds, the choir allowed the coffin and mourners to pass; and hastened by another road to the Church, where it met the funeral procession, and preceded it up the nave, singing the appointed sentences after Marbecke's notation. The Psalms were sung to the second tone; and after the Lesson, the procession left the Church, singing a hymn, 'How bright those glorious spirits shine.' At the conclusion of the Service, the bunch of flowers, which had before rested on the coffin, was laid on it again, and lowered with it into the grave[1]."

In this description, the vesting of the altar, the purple hangings of the apse, the pall with white and red crosses, the triangle of lights, and the use of the Psalm 'De profundis,' are all, with little variation, in accordance with Purchas' directions. But it will be asked, What is the meaning of the first and second celebrations? Upon this point also Mr. Purchas may throw some light. He remarks, 'The purpose for which of old the corpse was brought into the Church was to *have the Eucharistic sacrifice offered in the presence, and on behalf, of the dead.* He adds, When there is a *celebration of the Holy Eucharist* in the presence of the deceased, the Collect, 'O merciful God, the Father of our Lord Jesus Christ,' which occurs at the end of the Order of the Burial of the Dead as if it were an occasional prayer, is to be used in the

---

[1] Union Newspaper, Dec. 1857.

Communion Office instead of the Collect for the day. When there is no celebration, "the Collect" is a kind of link between the Burial of the Dead and the Eucharistic Office, and also the Church's protest for a *celebration on behalf of the soul of the deceased person.*'

A full exposure having now been made of the system upon which the St. Nicholas' Middle Schools were conducted, particular inquiries were set on foot by the Bishop of Rochester, who, it will be remembered, attended the Public Meeting in the Theatre, and the Vice-Chancellor, the issue of which appeared in the following, published in the Times and other newspapers,

" Correspondence relative to the Shoreham and Hurstpierpoint Middle Class Schools.

" *Danbury Palace, Chelmsford,*
Jan. 23, 1862.

" My dear Mr. Vice-Chancellor,

" Much time has elapsed since I had the honour of meeting you in the Theatre at Oxford, and of taking part in the proceedings over which you presided on behalf of St. Nicholas' College.

" In the interval, many representations, printed and otherwise, have reached me from friends; and I have been led to make extensive inquiries from the authorities of Hurstpierpoint, and from others.

" This proceeding has created in me the strongest distrust of the principles by which the Institutions are administered, and the practices which are encouraged or connived at in them.

"To my mind, it is obvious that distinctions of food and fasting are more than borne with, that something like particular confession is directly encouraged, and that practices, most incongruous with the teaching of a Reformed Church, are allowed in connexion with burials. Other things are told me, but it is needless for me to notice them.

"Under such circumstances, the part that I was led to take in your University is easily open to misrepresentation, and has been greatly misunderstood; and I am desirous to put myself right with the public and my friends.

"But before I do so, let me ask whether you are still satisfied in respect of these Institutions; or whether you have seen reason to alter the clear convictions in regard to them, which I then heard you express.

"It would be satisfactory to learn whether, if I make my present feelings on the subject known, I may add, in your own words, if you please, that you generally concur in them.

"Believe me, dear Mr. Vice-Chancellor,
"Yours very sincerely,
"J. C. ROCHESTER."

"*To the Rev. The Vice-Chancellor,*
Oxford."

"*Pembroke College, Oxford,*
"*Jan.* 25, 1862.

"My dear Lord,

"I have to acknowledge, with thanks, the receipt of your Lordship's letter of the 23rd inst.

"Like your Lordship, I have, since the Meeting in the Theatre in behalf of the Institutions to be connected with St. Nicholas, Shoreham, had to hear and to read much respecting the charges brought against the existing Schools in the anonymous handbill which I read to the Meeting; and I must not shrink from openly avowing, that I cannot now consider the charges in question to be 'mere myths,' as they were then, both in public and private, asserted to be.

"'Concurring' in your Lordship's views 'generally,' I must now suspend, and shall feel obliged, though with regret, wholly to withdraw my support of the excellent scheme of Mr. Woodard, unless, after a free and searching inquiry, it can be made evident that our distrust is without foundation.

"I am, my dear Lord,
"Your Lordship's faithful Servant,
"FRANCIS JEUNE."

"*The Right Rev. The Lord Bishop of Rochester.*"

A few days after the publication of this correspondence the author of the handbill received the following note from the Vice-Chancellor:

" *Pembroke College, Oxford,*
" *Feb.* 5, 1862.

" Dear Sir,—At a Meeting in the house of the Warden of All Souls' College on Monday last, which was attended by the Bishop of Oxford, the Dean of Christ Church, Professor Bernard, Mr. Medd, Captain Burrows, and myself, it was deemed advisable that a full and free inquiry should be made into the allegations which have been brought against St. Nicholas, Shoreham, and the institutions connected with it; and that the inquiry should be conducted by means of questions submitted to the Bishop of Chichester, with a request that he would obtain answers to them in his capacity of Visitor. The duty of preparing these questions was intrusted to a Committee, consisting of the Dean of Christ Church, the Warden of All Souls, Professor Bernard, and myself; and it was further agreed that I should transmit the questions to you, with the view that you might suggest any additions or emendations which you might think proper. The questions so prepared I now transmit to you, and remain,

" Dear Sir, yours faithfully,
" FRANCIS JEUNE.

" *The Rev. C. P. Golightly.*

" 1. What has been the greatest number of boys in each of the years 1859, 1860, 1861, in each of the Schools of Lancing, Hurstpierpoint, and Shoreham?

"II. Has confession in any form been used in any of these Schools within that period?

"III. If so,

"(a) How many boys have in each School and in each year confessed? To whom has the confession been made, and how often has each boy been received to confession?

"(b) State the ages of the boys who have confessed, their position in their respective Schools, and, so far as you can, their personal character.

"(c) Was the confession in every or in any case made by the boys *proprio motu*, or was it in any case advised or suggested by any Master, Chaplain, or other Officer in the Schools?

"(d) Were the boys left to state simply what was on their minds, or were they led on by questions put to them?

"(e) Has there been any stated or usual form or manner of making and receiving confession as regards words, posture, dress, or the place where confession was made?

"(f) Has confession been used only with a special view to the Holy Communion, or in cases of extreme sickness, or in any and in what other cases?

"(*g*) Has any kind or form of absolution or blessing been used in the cases specified in the preceding questions, or in other cases of confession, if any?

"(*h*) Has a boy who has once been received to confession been allowed in any case habitually or frequently to have recourse to it?

"(*i*) Has the practice of resorting to confession, or the tendency to resort to it, been an increasing practice or tendency, or a diminishing one, and to what extent?

"IV. Have beads or crucifixes been given or lent to any of the boys, in any of the Schools, by any of the Masters, Chaplains, or other Officers, or been allowed to be used by the boys?

"V. Is the description of the funeral given in the Union Newspaper, in December 1857, fair and accurate? If not, in what respects is it unfair or inaccurate? Has any such ceremony as is there described been used on any other occasion?

"VI. State distinctly what has been the rule or practice, if any, observed in any of the Schools with regard to the distinction of food on fast days.

"VII. Is it the fact that the Master, Chaplains, or other Officers of any of these Schools are, or have been, required to give a pledge or promise of 'silence as to whatever they may have noticed in the Institution?' If any thing like this has been done, state exactly for what reasons it was done, and within what limits."

The result of the inquiry was exceedingly curious. Mr. Woodard felt his dignity affronted by its 'free and searching character;' but what was he to do? It appears that his Schools are under the special patronage of the English Church Union, an association of which one of the objects is to support the Romanizing Clergy against their Bishops. A meeting° of the association was held, at which it was debated whether Mr. Woodard should be advised to answer 'a lengthy string of questions of so inquisitorial a character.' It was decided that he should do so, not however to Dr. Jeune and his colleagues, but to the Bishop of Chichester, who had already in the Theatre of

° At a meeting of the same society, an address to Mr. Woodard was carried by a considerable majority, in which he was assured that 'the great middle school movement, in which he had laboured so long and with such signal success,' was regarded by them 'as one of the most important that has marked this age of returning life to the English Church.' At the same meeting, a memorial to the Bishop of Rochester was *unanimously* adopted, in which it was pointed out to his Lordship, '*with high respect* (!!) *to his office as one of the chief pastors of the Church,*' that in his letter to Dr. Jeune, expressing distrust of Mr. Woodard's institutions, he had '*contradicted the Church's teaching*'!!

.Oxford pronounced the charges brought against Mr. Woodard to be 'myths'!! Mr. Woodard thought he could not do better than follow this considerate advice; but though the questions might have been answered in a fortnight, *the public heard no more about the matter for nearly two years.* Dr. Jeune's letter containing the questions is dated Feb. 5, 1862. In the Times, dated Oxford, Dec. 5, 1863, (when of course the public had utterly forgotten the point at issue,) there appeared the following notice:

" We, the undersigned, having prepared a set of questions designed thoroughly to sift the charges brought against the Schools connected with St. Nicholas College, Lancing, and having been allowed to transmit the questions, through *the Bishop of Chichester* as Visitor of the Schools, to the Managers, beg leave to report to those who may be interested in the matter, that *the Bishop considers,* from the answers received by him, *that the Schools are entirely exonerated from the charges brought against them.*

"S. Oxon.

"Henry G. Liddell, Dean of Christ Church, Oxon.

" Francis Jeune, Master of Pembroke.

" F. K. Leighton, Warden of All Souls, (Chairman and Treasurer of the Oxford Committee for Promoting the Erection of a Middle Class Public Boarding School.)

"Mountague Bernard, Chichele Professor of International Law, All Souls.

"Montagu Burrows, Chichele Professor of Modern History, All Souls.

"P. G. Medd, Secretary, University College."

The explanation of the above announcement is this : The answers to the questions addressed to Mr. Woodard were sent to the Bishop of Chichester, who declared himself satisfied, but *never reached Dr. Jeune and his colleagues at all*!! They *were not therefore in a position to give any opinion of their own upon them,* and surely *should have told the public so.* The reader must form his own judgment as to the fulfilment of the promise of " A FREE, FULL, AND SEARCHING INQUIRY."

At a public meeting held in January last at Burton on Trent, the Bishop of Lichfield in the chair, for the furtherance of a scheme for establishing a middle school at Denstone in Staffordshire, in connection with St. Nicholas College, Mr. Woodard announced that his Schools had still the support of the Bishop of Oxford. This, however, did not prevent the presentation of the following address to the chairman :

"To the Right Reverend John, Lord Bishop of Lichfield.

"We, the undersigned, inhabitants of Burton on Trent and its vicinity, in your Lordship's diocese, have heard with much concern that your Lordship did attend and preside at a meeting held at Burton, on Wednesday the 23rd ultimo, in support of the Rev. N. Woodard's designs of erecting a public school at Denstone in this County.

"We, thus addressing your Lordship, have the strongest reasons for believing that the doctrines taught, and practices encouraged, in the Schools already under the management of the Rev. N. Woodard and the Fellows of his Society, are not those of the United Church of England and Ireland as by law established. The system pursued under the management of the Rev. N. Woodard was some years since questioned and reproved by the Lord Bishop of the diocese, in which his already existing Schools are situated; and it still lies under the censure and disapprobation of the Bishops of Rochester and Peterborough, who have publicly withdrawn their countenance and support from the same.

"It is matter of common notoriety, and of which there can be no reasonable doubt, that the Rev. N. Woodard, and the promoters of his design, hold and profess the doctrines and opinions of those who, we are happy to believe, form an inconsiderable section of persons in the Church, and whose innovations and errors have been of late publicly censured and disclaimed in the Charges and Pastoral Addresses of nearly every one of your Lordship's most reverend and right reverend colleagues, the Archbishops and Bishops of the Church.

"We, now addressing your Lordship, have therefore much reason to fear that the great doctrines of the United Church of England and Ireland—'Justification by Faith only,' and 'that Holy Scripture containeth all things necessary to salvation, so that whatsoever is not read therein, or may be proved thereby, is not to be required of any man, that it should be believed as an article of the faith, or be thought requisite or necessary to salvation'—as set forth in the Articles of our Church, will not be prominently and faithfully taught in the religious instruction of the said proposed School; but that, on the contrary, a doctrine of justification by the *opus operatum* of the Sacraments, and of dependence upon human authority and tradition, will be inculcated instead, together with the practice of auricular confession, of ceremonies and usages, utterly abhorrent to the Protestant Church.

"We therefore humbly beg your Lordship to withdraw your countenance and support from the proposed School at Denstone, and ever to use your influence and authority in restraining all attempts to deprive us and our children of the inestimable benefits of the great Protestant Reformation. And so shall we ever remain your Lordship's faithful and obedient servants."

The above was signed by
16 Gentlemen,
17 Professional men, viz. Clergymen, Solicitors, Physicians, Surgeons, &c.
32 Brewers and Merchants,
526 Tradesmen, Farmers, Managers, and Clerks,
396 Artisans and workmen,
making a total of 987 signatures.

The Bishop of Oxford, at the public meeting in the Sheldonian Theatre, 'looked forward to the time when there would be on some healthy hill in the neighbourhood of Oxford a splendid College under Mr. Woodard.' But his hope has not yet been fulfilled.

"*Segnius irritant animos demissa per aurem,
Quam quæ sunt oculis subjecta fidelibus.*"

HOR. ARS POET.

S. OXON. ✠

"*Making himself look like a Roman Bishop.*"

CHURCH REVIEW.

THE LAST FEW MONTHS' EPISCOPATE.

A separate consideration, in illustration of the Bishop of Oxford's position in reference to Ritualism, will now be given to

CERTAIN FEATURES OF HIS EPISCOPATE DURING THE LAST FEW MONTHS.

These are, 1. His Authorized Photograph and Signature; 2. Advertisement in the Upper House of Convocation of 'The Church and the World;' 3. Presenting to the same House a petition from the English Church Union; 4. Sanctioning the introduction of a Stone Altar and Crucifix into Bloxham Church; 5. Suspension of the Rev. W. Acworth; and 6. Appointment of Dr. Pusey to preach at St. Mary's in Oxford.

1. *His Authorized Photograph and Signature.*

A photograph, representing him in the attitude of a Roman bishop, with his pastoral staff in one hand, and three fingers of the other lifted up in the act of blessing, (as symbolical of his authority from the Blessed Trinity,) having been commented upon by S. G. O. in the Times, Mr. Davenport, the Bishop's secretary, wrote thus in reply :

" The truth is, that the Bishop has been singularly importuned from time to time to sit for his photograph; and the one in question[a] was taken at the solicitation of friends, who suggested the introduction of the pastoral staff, while the posture of the Bishop is simply that which every Bishop occasionally assumes" (Mr. Davenport must be pardoned this slip, having been brought up a Dissenter) " when pronouncing a blessing."

The Bishop's signature is appended to an engraving taken from a picture not long since presented to him by several of his Clergy. It differs from Dr. Manning's only in the position of the cross, thus : ✠ H. E. Manning.—S. Oxon ✠.

2. Advertisement in the Upper House of Convocation of ' The Church and the World.'

The Romanizing party, in endeavouring to spread their opinions in the country, usually adopt what may be called the slow-poisoning system[b]; but in

[a] The Photograph is on sale at Messrs. Mowbray's, Oxford, price 1s. 6d.

[b] The following is an illustration, extracted from a letter in the Oxford Journal, from a parishioner of Banbury:

"We look around us, and see some of the village churches in our immediate neighbourhood "enlivened" by scenic decorations, childish processions with banners, choral services unintelligible to the poor and those who have no ear for music, and, what is far worse, the preaching of false doctrines; the disgusted parishioners informing us that *these innovations came on them gradually by little and little; ' this was nothing,' and ' that was nothing', until at length they are told ' it is too late to complain; they must bow to authority.'* "

the above work, framed upon the method of 'Essays and Reviews,' this course is abandoned. The strychnine is made up into bolusses, and vigorous efforts are made to force it down the patient's throat.

The reader, who may wish for a full account of this outrageous work, will find all that he can want to know in the article on Ultra-Ritualism in the Quarterly Review for Jan. 1867. But perhaps he will be satisfied with the following extracts:

(1.) *Protestantism.*

"Protestantism has produced all the heresy, and schism, and infidelity of the last 300 years, from Martin Luther to Joe Smith." p. 190.

(2.) *The Church of England.*

"Our place is appointed us among Protestants, and in a communion deeply tainted in its practical system by Protestant heresy; and our duty is, THE EXPULSION OF THE EVIL, NOT FLIGHT FROM IT." p. 237.

(3.) *The Thirty-nine Articles.*

"Protestant Articles tacked on to a Catholic Liturgy—those forty stripes save one, as some have called them, laid on the back of the Anglican priesthood—how are they to be got over? are they not a standing protest against every thing Roman? Doubtless we have been so taught, and most of us so believe." p. 202.

(4.) *Bishops.*

"The policy of the Prelates of the English Church has of late been one of oppression to the Catholic party. Courage in the cause of God and the Church is at present not the distinguishing character of her dignitaries; and it may be questioned whether, when a bill is introduced for the altering of the vestments of the priesthood, the episcopal mitre should not be abolished also, as antiquated, to make way for the more appropriate symbol of the white feather." p. 107.

(5.) *Need of Monastic Institutions.*

"Sisterhoods have long since become fixed institutions, and Monasteries will soon become equally common; we shall never again be without them." p. 247.

"Refounding religious houses[c], through the love

---

[c] It is a fact of Ecclesiastical History very little known, that Pope Paul III, in the year 1537, appointed a Commission of Cardinals and other dignified ecclesiastics to examine into the state of the Roman Church, and put down in writing what they considered ought to be reformed. One of their recommendations was, THE ABOLITION OF THE CONVENTUAL ORDERS. "Conventuales ordines abolendos esse putamus omnes."

The experience of William of Wykeham, (Bishop of Winchester 1367—1404,) as given at the 'Finis et Conclusio' of the New College Statutes, may serve to throw light on this recommendation. "We have in our days carefully examined the traditions of the ancient fathers, and the of our good Lord towards us, is become, perhaps, the most momentous work of our eventful days." p. 392.

After these few samples of the views advocated in this work, the reader will be not a little astonished at the following extract from the Chronicle of Convocation :

"UPPER HOUSE.
"Session XVII. Thursday, June 28, 1866.
" *The Church and the World.*
" The Bishop of Oxford.—I have now to present to your Grace, and this Upper House of Convocation, a book, which has been forwarded to me under cover, directed to the Upper House of Convocation. I have not read the book myself, but I venture to lay it upon the table, and ask you, if the House is pleased to receive it, that you will, with thanks to its presenter, allow it to be placed among your books of occasional reference. The work is entitled, *The Church and*

various approved rules of the saints, comparing with them the lives and conversation of those who profess to observe those traditions and rules; but it gives us pain to state, that nowhere now as formerly have we found the rules, statutes, and ordinances observed by their professors according to the intention of the Founders; for which cause we are greatly disturbed and confounded, finding how every where the darkness of night has obscured the clear light of day."

the World; or, Essays upon Questions of the Day. It is presented by the author to the Upper House of Convocation.

"The President[d].— Is it the pleasure of the House to receive it?

"The book was then laid upon the table without further remark.

"The Bishop of Salisbury.—I think we ought to present our thanks to the author of this book. *I have read a good many of the essays it contains, and they are most able. Although persons may differ from its conclusions, I am sure that every body, who takes the trouble of reading the work, will find a great deal of matter in it admirably well put together.*"

The advertisement (for such it was) by two Bishops of a work, the like of which had certainly never before issued from professed members of a Reformed Church, has been much commented upon. The language of the Bishop of Salisbury is painful and alarming. The Bishop of Oxford stated that he had not read the work: but is his judgment so easily surprised, that he should have been induced to present a book to Convocation which he had not so far looked into as to form a general idea of its contents? Was he not acting in concert with the Bishop of Salisbury, who 'had read a good many of the essays it con-

---

[d] i.e. the Archbishop of Canterbury.

tained,' and no doubt had imparted to his episcopal brother the opinion he had formed of their general character, as well as 'great ability?' The Bishop has since[e] pleaded that 'there was *no palpable impropriety in the book, such as to prevent his laying it upon the table*'!! It would have been more satisfactory, if he had expressed his great regret at his having been made the unconscious instrument of commending so disreputable a work to the notice of the public.

3. Presenting to the Upper House of Convocation a petition from the English Church Union.

One of the main objects of the English Church Union, as has been already observed, is to support the Romanizing Clergy against their Bishops; the society, in the event of legal proceedings, 'assuming every pecuniary liability arising therefrom.' At its annual meeting in June 1866, Dr. Pusey was elected a member of the Council by 571 votes, and a resolution was carried, all but unanimously, approving of his Eirenicon.

No more need be said by way of introduction to the following from the Chronicle of Convocation:

"UPPER HOUSE, JUNE 28, 1866.

"The Bishop of Oxford.—I have to present a petition from the Council of a body called the English Church Union, signed by their president,

[e] Upper House, Feb. 12, 1867.

and to be formally received as his only. [The Council prayed that, before the Upper House decided synodically against the use of vestments, incense, wafer-bread, &c. at the Holy Communion, they might be heard by counsel in favour of these practices.]

"The President.—Has such a prayer been ever granted?

"The Bishop of Ely.—Who signs it?

"The Bishop of Oxford.—It is signed, in behalf of the Council of the English Church Union, by the Hon. Colin Lindsay, as president.

"The Bishop of Ely.—Then it is his petition, in fact.

* * * * * *

"The Bishop of Oxford.—I presented the petition as the petition of Mr. Colin Lindsay. It is only in that way it can be received. *My Right Reverend brother seems to me to desire to shut out the moral weight which attaches to it as a petition signed in behalf of the Church Union.* It is true that by a convenient figment we receive it as the petition of Mr. Colin Lindsay; but we all know at the same time that it is the petition of a body of which that gentleman is president.

"The Bishop of Ely.—If the Church Union were a legally authorized body, we could of course receive its petition, signed by the president as representing that body. But, as I take it, this is a body of which we know nothing, and therefore the petition is to be received simply as the petition of Mr. Colin Lindsay.

"The Bishop of Oxford.—My Right Reverend brother is wrong in his law there. However authoritative the body itself may be, whose president has signed the petition, it is still the petition merely of the individual. *If my Right Reverend brother does not know any thing about the English Church Union, all I can say is, that he must be living in a somewhat remarkable state of ignorance of what is going on around him.*

"The Bishop of Ely.—I was aware of that point of law.... *With regard to the English Church Union, I beg to say that I do know a great deal about it, and that I wish I was in the happy state of ignorance respecting it to which the Bishop of Oxford refers.*

"The Bishop of Salisbury.—I think it undesirable that we should continue this discussion further. My Right Reverend brother the Bishop of Oxford has moved that the petition should lie upon the table, and that it be received as the petition of Mr. Colin Lindsay. But if we are going into a discussion of the character of the petition, and to consider whether or not it is *the petition of the Church Union*, perhaps some of us would wish to express an opinion with regard to that society; because *I am sure that all of us must agree, that some of the best members of the Church of England are connected with it.*"

4. The Sanctioning the introduction of a Stone Altar and Crucifix into Bloxham Church.

It will be borne in mind, that stone altars have been pronounced illegal by the Judicial Committee of the Privy Council, whose decisions, the Bishop maintains, are 'binding upon our consciences as Clergy, by our oaths and promises at ordination, licensing, and institution.'

In spite of this, at the reopening of Bloxham Church in November 1866, it appeared that in the Milcombe Chapelry of that Church '*the old altar had been restored, a new slab of Warwick stone, the gift of the architect, having been erected here on the old site.*' It is stated in the Record of the Diocese, in the Oxford Diocesan Calendar, that 'this chapelry is henceforth to be used for the daily matins and evensong, as also for early celebrations, (i.e. of the Sacrament of the Lord's Supper,) and on holy days.'

There are now, therefore, two *altars* (as the Ritualists term them) in this Church. Some years ago the Bishop justified the use of the cross in Churches, "as distinct from the Romish superstitions of the crucifix." But he makes no objection now either to stone altar or crucifix. Over the *high altar* on the reredos is 'a group of the crucifixion in white alabaster,' the effect of which has been thus described by a communicant: 'What struck my attention, when going up to the rails, was the

THE BLOXHAM CRUCIFIX.

alto-relievo of the reredos, which represented Christ on the cross, with the Virgin on one side, and St. John on the other. Though this was not a crucifix in the sense of one standing distinct from the altar behind it, to my notion it is really one; and I can not doubt that those persons who go to the Holy Communion, entertaining the belief of a local and corporal presence of Christ, will view that figure much as Romanists view the ordinary crucifix.'

At the luncheon which followed the reopening of the Church the Bishop made several short speeches, not one of which hinted at the slightest objection to any thing that had been done. On the contrary, 'when he looked upon that grand old Church, and compared it with what it had been, he thanked God for the work which they had been enabled to accomplish.' 'He must acknowledge the great services rendered by the Vicar of that place. He never would have been able to accomplish so much, but for the audacity of his noble daring, which had been blessed in their Church restoration and other respects with the greatest success.'

The 'success' of the Vicar may be judged of by the following from the Banbury Guardian: " RESULTS OF RITUALISM.—A Wesleyan Chapel, capable of holding upwards of 400 persons, is about to be erected in the populous village of Bloxham; *and many members of the Established*

Church, who cannot reconcile themselves to the manner in which the Church Services are now performed, contribute largely to the building fund."

5. The Suspension of the Rev. W. Acworth.

The Bishop of Oxford, in his Charge of December 1866, asks, 'How are the introducers of ritualistic rites to be treated by us? *Not, I venture to say at once, with harshness and reproach, not with unloving severity,* not with undistinguishing condemnation, not with unbrotherly suspicions. *These are not the weapons of Christian men; by these Christ's truth cannot be advanced.'*

A Romish service, 'the Improperia, or Reproaches,' having been introduced into St. Philip and St. James' Church in Oxford on Good Friday, 1866, the Rev. W. Acworth, an unbeneficed clergyman temporarily residing in Oxford, complained to the Bishop through the Archdeacon. The answer of the Archdeacon, which conveyed no message from the Bishop, being thoroughly unsatisfactory, Mr. Acworth next addressed a public letter to the Archbishop of Canterbury. Two days only after its publication Mr. Acworth received the following inhibition from the Bishop of Oxford:

"*Cuddesdon, May* 25, 1866.

"Rev. Sir,—I withdraw the permission I gave you to officiate in this diocese, and require you to surcease from doing so until you have obtained a renewed permission from me.

"I remain yours truly,

"*Rev. W. Acworth.*" "S. Oxon."

It has been the object of the writer in the foregoing pages rather to inquire what the Bishop's views are in reference to Ritualism, than to find fault with him for holding them; but he must needs maintain that, in his treatment of Mr. Acworth, he was guilty of a grave moral offence, greatly aggravated by the consideration that his right of permitting or refusing permission to a clergyman to preach the Gospel in his diocese was given him for a totally different purpose to that of avenging a supposed personal affront.

6. The appointing Dr. Pusey to preach at St. Mary's in Oxford.

When Mr. Newman published the celebrated Tract XC, the object of which was to show that it was possible to subscribe the Thirty-nine Articles, and yet believe the doctrines of Trent; in other words, hold Protestant preferment together with Romish opinions; his publication was condemned by the Board of Heads of Houses and Proctors in the following terms:

"Resolved, That modes of interpretation, such as are suggested in the said Tract, evading rather than explaining the sense of the Thirty-nine Articles, and reconciling subscription to them, with the adoption of errors which they were designed to counteract, defeat the object, and are inconsistent with the due observance of the Statutes of this University.

"P. WYNTER,
"*Vice-Chancellor.*"

Not long after the appearance of this 'grave and well-considered document,' the Bishop of the diocese (Bishop Bagot) pronounced the system of interpretation advocated in Mr. Newman's Tract 'so subtle, that by it the Articles might be made to mean any thing or nothing.' The present Bishop, although remarking (Charge, Dec. 1866, p. 42) that the Tract had met with ' the general condemnation of the episcopal body,' pronounces no opinion upon it of his own, but has within the last few weeks appointed Dr. Pusey, *who in spite of the condemnation of the Bishops has recently reprinted the Tract*, to preach at St. Mary's in Oxford.

But Dr. Pusey has advocated views at utter variance with those of his Lordship on other important points, viz. the Eucharist, and Auricular Confession.

THE EUCHARIST.

Dr. Pusey maintains that ' the Council of Trent, *whatever its look is,* and our Articles, *whatever their look,* can be so explained, as to reconcile one with another.'

Let this position be tested on the point of Transubstantiation:

Church of England.	Rome.
Art. XXVIII.	*Council of Trent, Sess.* XXII. *Canon 2.*
"Transubstantiation, or the change of the substance of bread and wine in the Supper of the Lord, cannot be proved by Holy Writ; but is repugnant to the plain words of Scripture, overthroweth the nature of a Sacrament, and hath given occasion to many superstitions."	"If any one saith, that in the Sacred and Holy Sacrament of the Eucharist the substance of the bread and wine remains conjointly with the Body and Blood of our Lord Jesus Christ, and denieth that wonderful and singular conversion of the whole substance of the bread into the Body, and of the whole substance of the wine into the Blood—the species only of the bread and wine remaining—which conversion indeed the Catholic Church most aptly calls Transubstantiation, let him be anathema."

It must be admitted that the above documents 'look' very unlike, and that it would require all the ingenuity of Dr. Pusey and Mr Newman so to 'explain them as to make them reconcile one with another.' But let the reader set the following statement of Dr. Pusey's side by side with the

Tridentine Canon, and he will see that the likeness is unmistakeable:

"I believe, that in the Holy Eucharist the Body and Blood of Christ are sacramentally, supernaturally, ineffably, but verily and indeed, present under the form of bread and wine,' and that ' where His Body is, *there* is Christ[f].' "

But what can be more unlike the view maintained[g] by the Bishop of Oxford? " Nothing can be clearer than the declaration of our great Reformers, as they are embodied in our formularies. They maintain beyond all controversy the doctrine of our Lord's spiritual presence in His holy Sacrament; they *utterly deny any change whatever of substance in the consecrated bread and wine*, OR ANY CORPORAL OR LOCAL PRESENCE AS ACCOMPANYING THE ELEMENTS. This plain statement of this great truth I thank God I altogether receive, and hold, and enforce, without equivocation or subterfuge, and *from* it I would not consent that there should be taken, nor *to* it added, one iota."

AURICULAR CONFESSION.

Bishop of Oxford.	*Dr. Pusey.*
" I hold that the Church of England discountenances any attempt on the part of her Clergy to introduce a	" Mr. Dodsworth knew, *as I know*, that to say merely that you have *encouraged* Confession, would

[f] Sermon on John vi. 67—69. p. 26.
[g] Supra, p. 8.

system of habitual Confession, or, in order to carry out such a system, to require men and women to submit themselves to the questioning and examination of the priest. Such a system of inquiry into the secrets of hearts must, in my judgment, lead to innumerable evils. GOD FORBID THAT OUR CLERGY SHOULD ADMINISTER, OR THAT OUR WIVES AND DAUGHTERS SHOULD BE SUBJECTED TO IT." *Supra,* p. 7.

fall as far short of what your actual practice is, as the word '*enjoin*' in the sense of compelling would exceed it. He knew that you have done more than encouraged confession in very many cases; that you have warned people of the danger of deferring it, have insisted on it as the only remedy, have pointed out the inevitable dangers of the neglect of it, and have promised the highest blessings in the observance, until you had BROUGHT PENITENTS IN FEAR AND TREMBLING ON THEIR KNEES BEFORE YOU." *Maskell's Letter to Pusey.*

Mr. Maskell, a quondam disciple of Dr. Pusey's, is now a Romanist. The letter quoted was written in 1850. In another part of it he charges Dr. Pusey with ' secretly receiving persons against the known will of their parents, hearing confessions in the houses of common friends, and with clandestine correspondence to arrange meetings, under initials, or in envelopes addressed to other persons.'

The Bishop of Oxford himself, in his Charge of 1851, severely animadverted on certain publications of Dr. Pusey's, as calculated to produce secession to

Rome; viz. Romish books of devotion professedly adapted to the use of the Church of England. 'Not only had language been preserved in them alien from the sober teaching of the Church of England, and in harmony only with the half-amatory devotions in which Rome so largely abounds, but *even the direct corruptions of the Papacy had not always been successfully excluded.*' It was accordingly 'his full conviction that the circulation and use of these works, many of which were originally composed and circulated purposely to counteract the Reformation, has had, and still has, a most dangerous influence in this direction.'

The Bishop added in a note: " The Romanists are well aware of this. A recent writer of their communion, referring to Dr. Pusey's adaptations, says, 'For one whom our books of controversy have brought round, at least twenty have yielded to the power of our devotions.'"

Yet this dangerous writer the Bishop was not afraid to put into St. Mary's pulpit, with the certain knowledge that a large proportion of his hearers would be Undergraduates of the University!

THE CHARGE OF DECEMBER 1866.

FULL thirty pages of this Charge are taken up with an apology for Ritualism. Whilst occupying the position of a judge, the Bishop adopts the language of an advocate. 'An Oxford priest', writing the day after its delivery to the Church Review, which the reader will bear in mind is one of the chief organs of the ultra-Ritualistic party, remarks upon it: " The Bishop of Oxford's Charge, which I heard yesterday, is too important to be treated of at the end of a letter. It is enough for the present to say, that, with whatever shortcomings, there is a general feeling in this place (i. e. among the Ritualistic party) that it is *one for which as a whole we have reason to be deeply grateful.*" The Editor of the Church Review regarded it as 'a matter of congratulation to the Catholic party,' who had in the Bishop of Oxford one 'who possessed an intelligent sympathy with the revival, not merely in its accidents, but in its true spiritual character.'

A perusal of the Charge will shew that this is a just estimate of its contents.

In the first place, the Bishop flings to the winds all that he had said in 1859 to his Archdeacons and Rural Deans, in reference to 'Facts and Documents,' about his "utter disapproval of all attempts to introduce unusual Ritualistic developements, and the danger of the Clergy wasting their own energies, and estranging the hearts of their people, by giving themselves up to such childish frivolities." The movement which originated with Mr. Newman, and has carried over to Rome some two thousand of his followers, is now in his judgment a movement from God. Their teachers were ready to fight 'the good fight to which THE VOICE had called them.' It was a movement '*mighty for good,* in spite of all its drawbacks.' Out of it had arisen 'this great developement of Ritualism.' " How were the introducers of the newly-restored rites to be treated by us? Not with harshness and reproach, not with unloving severity." (No, such treatment was to be reserved for their opponents.) " Amongst the Clergy and Laity, who are conspicuous for the introduction of these novelties, are men inferior to none in self-devotion, in apparent love to Christ, in tenderness towards the poor, in zeal for His truth, or in the fervour of their own devotion. *Such men we can ill afford to lose.*" Yet somehow or other we are in danger of losing them. How so? Why, if the truth must be told, these excellent men are more than half way to Rome already, and are in danger of following the example of Mr. Newman and Dr. Manning in turning Romanists quite, unless they are allowed to indulge their Ritualistic fancies in the Church of England. There is no other way of accounting for the danger. Opposition does not make people Romanists. The shaking of the apple-tree may bring down the ripe fruit, but has no tendency to ripen it. The Bishop "trusts that no taunts from without, and no timorousness within, will lead any of the rulers of their Church" (this is surely giving his Episcopal brethren a very indifferent character) "to aid in driving out any one who can consistently with truth and faithfulness be kept among us, lest we repeat again our fathers' fault, and lose our brethren, as they lost John Wesley and his noble fellows."

This last argument, which occurs more than once in 'The Church and the World,' (pp. 98, 350,) is thus replied to in the article on Ultra-Ritualism in the Quarterly Review:

"The Ritualists are fond of warning us against repeating towards them the error which was committed by the authorities of our Church in the case of Wesley; and others, as Dean Stanley, repeat the warning, although they do greater justice to the Bishops of that time. But the parallel fails in two points,—that Wesley professed a warm affection for the Church, which these men invariably vituperate; and that whereas Wesley and his brethren, in so far as they were thrust out of the Church, were thrust out by the personal acts of the Bishops, the Ritualists, if they are to suffer, will suffer from legal judgments. Their movement, as has been truly said, 'is not a defensive movement, not a movement on the side of liberty, but an aggressive one;' the attempt of a small knot of men, unknown except for their extravagances, to revolutionize the system which has been settled among us for more than three hundred years."

A long time elapsed between the delivery of the Bishop of Oxford's Charge and its publication. The reason of the delay did not appear; but no doubt the Bishop felt it an embarrassing circumstance, that, his Charge being mainly an echo of the Report of the Lower House of Convocation on Ritualism, his arguments in favour of the Ritualists had been by anticipation torn to tatters in the Bishop of St. David's unsparing criticism of that most misleading document. It would be curious to see, side by side, the one Bishop's arguments and the other's replies. One or two extracts from their respective Charges will suffice to shew how widely they differ in their views of the tendency of the Ritualistic movement; and probably by this time the reader will readily form his own judgment as to which Bishop is right.

Bishop of Oxford.

"Should it at last unhappily be plain that any do *indeed intend,* through practices at least somewhat assimilated to those of Rome, *to introduce the Roman teaching,*" (i.e. in plain violation of their Ordination vow, '*so to minister the Doctrine and Sacraments, and the discipline of Christ,* as the Lord hath commanded, and *as this Church and Realm hath received the same*[a],') " one course, and one course only, as to them would then remain. May God avert that evil day, and teach us in the mean time how to draw closer to ourselves *those whom, for our very love of* HIM WHOM THEY LOVE, we cannot choose but love !

" Most reluctantly should I admit any general charge of disloyalty to our own Church, as the moving spring of this Ritual developement. In some few of its abettors such disloyalty may lurk,— I trust in very few. I cannot doubt the hearty honesty of the great number of those whose actions I am nevertheless compelled to condemn. *I desire to believe that they have intended only to protest in act against the careless negligence which has shocked them in some of their brethren, and against the lowering down, through modern unbelief, of some of the great doctrines of our reformed communion; that they have desired to raise the English, not to introduce the Romish use.*"

BISHOP OF ST. DAVID'S.

" This Ritual movement has by no means reached its term. It is still in the full vigour of its early years. It appears to be advancing, both extensively in the work of proselytism, and

[a] See Ordination Service.

intensively in doctrinal innovation; not always distinctly enunciated, but clearly intimated. Its partisans seem to vie with one another in the introduction of more and more startling novelties, both of theory and practice. The adoration of the consecrated wafer, reserved for that purpose, which is one of the most characteristic Romish rites, and a legitimate consequence of the Romish Eucharistic doctrine, is contemplated, if it has not been already adopted, in some of our Churches; and the Romish festival of the *Corpus Christi,* instituted for the more conspicuous exercise of that adoration, has, it appears, actually begun to to be observed by Clergymen of our Church. Already public honours are paid to the Virgin Mary, and language applied to her, which can only be considered as marking the first stage of a developement, to which no limit, short of the full Romish worship, can be probably assigned[b].

"I believe that on the main point I have said nothing but what is universally known; and I should not be surprised, if there were many who will smile at the pains I have been taking to light a candle in the broad day to help them to see what is so patent to all. I should myself have thought it a superfluous labour, if I had not observed in some quarters an appearance of a tacit agreement to treat the fact as a kind of

[b] Charge, p. 104.

sacred mystery, familiar indeed to the initiated, but not to be divulged to the profane. I can be no party to a system of concealment, which appears to me neither manly nor perfectly consistent with good faith, or with a plain duty to the Church; and I regard the prevalence of such a system as one of the least honourable and the most ominous signs of our time.

"Nothing in my judgment can be more mischievous, as well as in more direct contradiction to notorious facts, than to deny or ignore the Romeward tendency of the movement^c."

No feature of the Bishop of Oxford's Charge is more painful than the absence of all distinct censure of Dr. Pusey's republication of Tract XC.

The writer of these pages was once intimate with the author of that Tract, and looked up to him with high respect. Nearly, *but not quite, the first* shock to his confidence in him was his meeting with the following passage in his 'Arians of the Fourth Century':

"The Alexandrian father, (Clement,) who has already been referred to, *accurately describes the rules which should guide the Christian in speaking and acting economically.* 'Being ever persuaded of the Omnipresence of God,' he says, 'and ashamed to come short of the truth, he is satisfied with the approval of God, and of his own conscience.

^c Charge, pp. 114, 115.

Whatever is in his mind is also on his tongue; towards those who are fit recipients, both in speaking and living, he harmonizes his profession with his opinions. *He both thinks and speaks the truth, except when consideration is necessary, and then, as a physician for the good of his patients, he will be false, or utter a falsehood, as the Sophists say*[d].'"

He remonstrated with Mr. Newman both in conversation and writing, but he tried to get rid of his objections by a joke; 'I abandon Clemens Alexandrinus to your tender mercies, &c.' He remembers to have called the attention of the Hon. and Rev. Arthur Perceval, one of the originators of the Tractarian movement, to the passage, and that he turned away from it in disgust. 'Yes,' he said, 'I know that several of the early fathers express themselves in that manner, and it is by appealing to such passages that the Jesuits justify pious frauds.'

Can it be questioned that Tract XC. is a developement of the Alexandrian father's principle, and that it is framed upon the rules ' which should guide the Christian in speaking and acting economically?' There is no doubt that its effects upon the Ritualistic Clergy have been most demoralizing, and that many have been 'emboldened' by it to sign what they did not believe. Let the reader look again at the extract given (supra, p. 61) from 'The Church and the World,' relative to the

[d] Arians, p. 81.

Thirty-nine Articles: " Protestant Articles tacked on to a Catholic Liturgy—those forty stripes save one, as some have called them, laid on the back of the Anglican priesthood—how are they to be got over?" Here we have the unhappy Ritualist scrutinizing our Church's formularies, like a pettifogging attorney intent upon driving a coach and four through an Act of Parliament. Is there no monitor within to whisper to him, Better cut off your right hand, than subscribe what you do not believe? ' Better enter into life halt or maimed, &c.' Hearken to one misled for a time, but enabled at length to break through the net which an ingenious sophistry had wound round him. *" Not one of us but must own it; not one but has writhed under the torture of doubting whether on the threshold of this system, which he embraces to make him holy, there rests not the stain and semblance of a lie.* Is this too harsh a term? But what is the fact? Do we not, as Catholics, claim to believe doctrines which yet we dare not avow in their plain unmistakeable words? We dare not; for alas! the Church of England does not give us plain and unmistakeable words in which to avow them; and *if we convince ourselves that she does not rather intend us to avow* THEIR VERY REVERSE, *it is only by a course of explanation which twists her apparently most Protestant statements into a positive sanction of Catholic truth.*" Again, " We tread the aisle with faltering steps, trying to do as we are bid, and to drown our doubts with *clever prevarications*. We see the priest stand before the altar... It is as if he said, 'I am here offering up the sacrifice of the very Body and Blood of Christ for the remission of quick and dead. But it is a secret between you and me: I could not teach the people so; it would give offence, seeming contrary to the Prayer-book, though in reality it is not, *because the Article which denies it is not aimed at the doctrine itself, but at the particular way in which once it was taken by the vulgar....* You may adore, for you see everybody kneels; *and though the Church of England says it is idolatry to do so, she meant exactly the reverse;* or, if she did not actually command it, she at any rate permits her children to do what her language calls idolatrous.'" "Wonderful sophistry! most solid ground of faith! excellent school for guilelessness and sincerity! admirable preparation for making men good, and saintly, and christian, *except perhaps making them true*!" "Is not every article of belief choked with a sophism?" "We prevaricate and evade, and get out of difficulties in a manner *worthy of those whose rule of faith is the Catholic interpretation which Tractarianism puts on the Prayer-book and Articles of our Reformed Church*[e]."

[e] The author is indebted for the whole of this passage to the Dean of Ripon's very valuable work, 'Rome's Tactics.' (Hatchard and Co.) The Dean quotes it from a pamphlet,

Against this demoralizing system the Bishop of Oxford's Charge contains no distinct word of warning. 'Many powers,' he tells us, 'our Church has lodged in its living governors. It is their charge to interpret ambiguous rubrics, to reduce to unity matters diversely taken, to acquiesce in or to disallow changes which by minute accretions the living body has silently developed.' But has not our Church laid upon her 'living governors' a more solemn duty still? Witness the words of her Ordinal at the Consecration of Bishops:

"*The Archbishop.*

"Are you ready, with all faithful diligence, to banish and drive away all erroneous and strange doctrines contrary to God's Word; and both privately and openly to call upon and encourage others to do the same?

"*Bishop.*
" I am ready, the Lord being my helper."

The Diocese is in a very agitated state. Alarming rumours circulate even in the most remote villages, to the effect that the Church of England is going back to Rome. At Bloxham, as has been already

entitled, 'The Morality of Tractarianism: a Letter, from one of the People to one of the Clergy.' London, Pickering, 1850.

seen, a Wesleyan Chapel, capable of containing 400 persons, is about to be erected; and *many members of the Established Church*, who cannot reconcile themselves to the manner in which the Church Services are now performed, *are contributing largely to the Building Fund.* It appears, from a recently published correspondence between the Bishop and one of the principal inhabitants (Mr. Fortescue), that several members of the congregation of the *Parish* Church of Banbury ' have already joined dissenting congregations;' and that others are likely to follow their example, if certain alterations recently made in the Services are persisted in. Lastly, the following Lay Declaration, which there is reason to believe expresses the feelings of a large proportion of the middle classes both in towns and villages, was in March last presented to the Bishop by 200 male Communicants of Reading :

" *To the Right Reverend the Lord Bishop of Oxford.*

" My Lord,—In the year 1859, as it will be recollected by your Lordship, an Address, signed by four thousand lay members of the Church of England in the Diocese of Oxford, (including three Members of Parliament, twenty-three Magistrates, and one hundred and seventy-nine Churchwardens,) was presented to your Lordship, expressing the existence ' in the minds of the best friends of our

Church of a growing mistrust, in consequence of the Romanizing tendency of many of the innovations recently introduced by certain of the Clergy into the practices and ritual of its services;' and praying your Lordship, 'in virtue of your office, to arrest the progress of these objectionable innovations, to allay the fears entertained, and to suppress all such causes for further apprehension.'

"We, the undersigned residents in Reading, (being lay Communicants of the Reformed Church of England as by law established, and many of whose signatures were attached to the Address above referred to,) not only feel that that Address has failed to accomplish its wished-for results, but we are deeply impressed with the sad conviction, shared we believe in common with a very large number of our fellow-countrymen, that a widespread apostacy from Protestant truth and practice has already taken place in our land, and that in the Diocese over which your Lordship so energetically presides the evil is extensively diffused and actively progressing.

"To your Lordship's long recognised sympathies and acts in favour of what is popularly designated the 'High Church system,' we do not doubt that such a lamentable result is to be greatly, though not exclusively, ascribed.

"In your Lordship's elaborate, but in our judgment singularly ambiguous and unsatisfactory Charge of December last, you congratulate the

Diocese on its freedom from 'Ritualistic extravagances.'

"We must respectfully demur to the accuracy of this statement. But even admitting the outward manifestation of ultra-Ritualism to be comparatively rare, we are deeply persuaded that in no Diocese is there greater preponderance of that doctrinal teaching, of which Ritualism is nothing more than the natural fruit and expression.

"It is true that in the Charge referred to 'extreme Ritualism' is gravely rebuked; that Rome is declared to be the 'oldest and deadliest enemy' of the Church of England, and all attempts at union with Rome are strongly denounced; but the definition of what Ritualism really consists, or of the doctrines from which it springs, and 'of which rites are the shadows,' is nowhere to be found; while in other of your Lordship's remarks you appear to re-build the things you had just before been destroying, and re-establish the very principles which it seemed your intention to condemn.

"We deem it right, therefore, publicly to give expression to our opinions, being satisfied that they will be re-echoed by a large number of the reflecting lay members of the Church of England in this Diocese and elsewhere; and wishing your Lordship to be aware that, instead of that 'harmony' which, 'to a degree rare at this time almost every where,' is said in your Charge to abound, wide-spread distrust and apprehension really exist.

"Under these circumstances, after close observation of your Lordship's Episcopal career, and impelled by the deep conviction that the present is the most important religious crisis which has come upon England since the Reformation, we feel it our bounden but painful duty respectfully, yet frankly, to state that we have no confidence in the course pursued by your Lordship as our Spiritual Guide."

CONCLUSION.

A distinguished French Protestant writer, Merle d'Aubigné, has compared the Church of England struggling with her present difficulties to a gallant ship among the breakers. Certain it is that the ship no longer obeys the helm, and seems to be drifting nearer and nearer towards the shallows. But, perhaps, a still more appropriate comparison would be that of a besieged city, of which part of the garrison have mutinied; some have already gone over to the enemy, others are watching for an opportunity of opening the gates[a] to him. Worst

---

[a] Let the reader ponder the following words of an ultra-Ritualist writer in the Church Review:

"I cannot but think that Lord Ardmillan has taken a more enlarged view of the Ritual movement than many of our Bishops, *including my Lord of St. David's*. He clearly sees what it all means, and has read the most modern manifestos of the school, including 'The Church and the World.' He sees that, if this party triumphs, the Protestantism of the Church of England is gone. This, of course, from his point of view he deprecates. He really fears that *nothing but a great uprising can save the Church of England from being un-Protestantized, its Articles abandoned, and a reunion effected between the three bodies which claim to themselves the name of Catholics and the possession of the Priesthood.* DOUBTLESS NO LESS IS AT STAKE."

of all an officer, high in command, whilst making the strongest professions of his own loyalty, takes every opportunity of expressing his sympathy with the mutineers; pleads their cause at head quarters, claims for them credit for the best intentions, bestows the highest marks of confidence upon their leaders, is looked upon by them as their best friend, and, what is still more remarkable, has adopted the sign manual of one of the enemy's marshals, and has had his picture taken, not indeed in a marshal's uniform, but with the fingers of his right hand uplifted in the favourite attitude of those officers on parade, and with his left hand grasping a baton. A subordinate complaining of the proceedings of some of the mutineers, he cashiered him on the spot.

The Church of England is at the present moment a house divided against itself; and, as in the days of Lord Clarendon, there is 'a schism among the Bishops,' one of whom—would to God we could confidently say he were the only one—gives his whole 'power and strength' to the Romeward movement. To borrow the language of Lord Shaftesbury, at the great County Meeting at Dorchester, "our position is painful in the extreme. It is not an enemy that hath done this, but, as we may say, our own familiar friend. It has come from one with whom we might have taken sweet counsel, to whom we look for guidance and protection, to whom we looked to drive away all erroneous doctrine and all evil from the Church of which we are members. I say it has come from our own familiar friend, and from him whom we may almost call our natural protector."

Now what will be the issue of all this? We are reminded by the highest authority that 'a house divided against itself cannot stand.' In proportion as Romish principles spread among the Clergy, the hearts of the people of England will be more and more alienated from the National Church. The Bishop of St. David's[b] anticipates 'large secessions, perhaps of whole congregations, to the ranks of dissent.' The experience of the Bishop of St. Asaph[c] is, that Ritualism is now 'driving away the middle orders from our parish Churches.' The Bishop of Llandaff[d], speaking as a Welsh Bishop, is of opinion, that it 'will throw back the work of the Church in the principality a hundred years.' The Bishop of London 'is certain that, if this evil goes on, the number of parishes will be very great where the laity will be of one form of religion, and the parish priest, with his acolytes and thurifers, of another.' The Bishop of Winchester, so far from agreeing with his brother of Oxford in regarding the movement as one 'mighty for good,' is of opinion, that the Ritualistic observances are 'acting to a very dangerous extent on the attachment of the intelligent laity to the Church. They cause

[b] Charge, p. 117.   [c] Chronicle of Convocation, p. 148.
[d] Ibid. p. 155.

not divisions only, but alienation. Irritation and angry feelings are excited, and end in secession.'

Is not all this what happened in the days of Laud?

And yet, in spite of the Ritualistic movement, never, since the introduction of Christianity into the island, has more work been done for God by the National Church.

The Ritualists never cease to rail at the Bishops. But perhaps at no period of our Church's history has there ever been at the same moment a greater number of eminent men on the Bench, or the character of the Bishops stood higher. Seldom have we had prelates of greater intellectual power than the Archbishop of York, and the Bishops of St. David's, Exeter, and Peterborough; or of more untiring energy and devotedness than the Bishops of Norwich, Durham, and Carlisle. The zeal and liberality of the parochial Clergy, evidenced by the sacrifices which they make in the cause of education, and in the building and restoring of Churches, are beyond all praise. It is a fact which has been hardly noticed, that more than one in twelve of all the Churches in England, i.e. 1,200 out of 14,000, were erected between the years 1841 and 1851[e], in the very decade, strange to say, in which Mr. Newman and so many of his followers forsook the Church of England for Rome.

[e] See Prefatory Account, supra, p. iii.

Why then has this distress come upon us?

The writer will not be deterred by any apprehension of rationalistic and sceptical sneers from expressing his conviction that it is the result of more than human agency, even of the secret working of him who, as the Scripture warns us, is able to transform himself into an angel of light, and his ministers into ministers of righteousness.

This was the view of one to whose wisdom and energy the Church of England is deeply indebted, the late Bishop Blomfield[f]:

"For my own part, I cannot doubt but that the great spirit of evil, the prince of the power of this world, who looks 'with jealous leer malign' upon the Reformed Church of England, as destined, it may be, and called upon by her singular opportunities and means, to be the evangelizer of the world, and the chosen instrument of beating down his strongholds, and carrying forward into his dominions the kingdom of the Redeemer, is using special efforts to weaken her capacities of good, and regarding with complacency those intestine divisions, which prey upon her vitals, and tend to paralyse her powers of action."

And if the evil is to be traced to this cause, we need be at no loss where to look for the remedy. Most imploringly would the writer appeal to those of his brethren among the Clergy and Laity, who

[f] Memoir, vol. ii. p. 188.

believe that prayer moves the hand that moves the world, to address themselves to the task, with the utmost seriousness and earnestness, of interceding fervently day and night, in the first place, for our brethren in error, that it may please God to shew them the light of His truth; and next, that He, who ' has done so great things for us already,' may yet 'make our Jerusalem a praise upon earth,' by enabling her to bring forth more and more fruit to the glory of His great name, through Jesus Christ our Lord.

THE END.

www.ingramcontent.com/pod-product-compliance
Lightning Source LLC
Chambersburg PA
CBHW031349160426
43196CB00007B/789